If I was cajoled to rule

by

Dipo Otuyemi

This printed version or the book version is published in October 2019

Email: dipo_otuyemi@yahoo.com

Facebook: https://www.facebook.com/dipo.otuyemi

Twitter: @dipo_otuyemi

#ifiwascajoledtorule

<u>About the Author</u>

Mr Dipo Otuyemi is a built environment professional with wide ranging experience worldwide in the public, not-for-profit and private sectors of the built environment. He is a graduate of OAU, Ile-Ife, Nigeria and holds a postgraduate qualification from the Southbank University, London UK. His major interest extends to innovations in ICT and he has seeded a number of ICT innovative start-ups and currently developing, in conjunction with some ICT experts, other innovations in the ICT sector which are expected to be mainstreamed into popular culture and our day-to-day Internet-of-things intertwined lives in the nearest future. He currently runs a management and consultancy firm that specialize in construction, facilities (including ICT) and infrastructural developments.

He is a keen badminton and basketball player.

Table of Content

-Civil service (general)
-Public service
-Housing
-Health
-Education
-Commerce & Industry
-Employment generation
-Agriculture
-Environmental
-Urban renewal & regeneration
-Transportation & Roads
-Power
-Water
-ICT
-Existing/Legacy Infrastructures
-Security
-IGR (Internally Generated Revenue)
-Social Services and Welfare
-Legal/Legislative Framework
-PPP ROI Guarantee
-Personnel Transfer and Other
 Undertakings
-SLAs, KPIs etc.
-Regulatory bodies for PPP by sector
-Employment & Contracting Local Content
 Law
-Building Laws & Regulations
-Environmental Laws
-Transport/Traffic laws
-Maintenance of State Asset
-Health and Safety
-Disability, OAP etc. Discrimination and
 Associated laws
-Data Protection

PROLOGUE

'If I was cajoled to rule' metamorphosed from personal thoughts, previous submissions and discussions with other Nigerians and non-Nigerians alike about the seemingly insurmountable problems that has stunted the growth of the most populous black nation, with abundance of natural resources, into the global giant and economic powerhouse that the whole world expected it to have achieved a couple of decades ago.

The book is not a scholastic work output neither does it present any heavy reading by any standard, if anything, it should present a lightweight reading across the board to varying level and/or degree of readers.

It looks at the underlying human problems from the street level to the failure of the political and other sectional leadership who have consistently failed the nation in productive and sustainable governance for decades.

It is an insight into Nigeria that most Nigerians are aware of but will fail to admit to themselves because of acquired 'collective self-denial' that most Nigerians are well known for, hence, it will be a good read and eye-opener for objective and subjective Nigerians alike; and indeed, an interesting read for all the black people throughout the globe for introspection as they will see an element of themselves somehow mirrored in the make-up of Nigerians. It will also serve as a good guide majorly for non-blacks too that have to either deal or interact with Nigerians and other blacks, both within the continent and in the diaspora. It offers a roadmap to the average Nigerian mind and thought process without actually demystifying the sanctity of the Nigerian mind;

that is left for the readers to achieve or decipher on their own tailwind.

The policy proposals in the latter part of this book, although geared towards the political class (leaders and followers) as an impetus for critical thinking in terms of policy conception and development, are not exhaustive neither are they recommended as panacea for the myriads of developmental issues facing the nation. They are elementary and off-the-cuff policies which policy makers can develop and build on to ensure a more egalitarian Nigerian society and in the process correct some malady in the inequality and perceived injustice pervading the Nigerian political and socio-economical space/landscape.

CHAPTER ONE -The Leaders, Followers and their Beliefs

The Leaders

The political class who are the undisputed leaders of the Nigerian people are really a peculiar lot; mostly greedy, selfish and egocentric. One will have to acknowledge a pocket here and there of decent, truly altruistic and benevolent politicians, but they are few and far between.

In Nigeria, to be elected into a political post, and hence become a leader, is deemed to be an automatic ticket for personal enrichment and aggrandizement at the expense of the masses.

I was in a conundrum as to what title to give to this chapter, leaders or elites? Of course in Nigeria, as in some other nations, Nigeria is not short of its sectorial, political, traditional, cultural, ethnic, religious etc. leaders who are looked up to reverently by their respective followers. While elite connotes a class or caste system which may be hereditary in nature, hence not earned, a leader on the other hand is deemed to be classless and achievable by hard work, luck or enthronement.

As leaders being referenced majorly in this chapter are the political leaders who are tasked by the populace by their electoral choices to rule the nation and chart a safe and economically viable course for the Nigerian nation, I assumed 'leaders' is aptly suited rather than 'elites'. To my consternation, my choice was almost jettisoned when a friend who was newly elected as a member of his state house of assembly boastfully told a couple of friends and me that he had now joined the Nigerian elites. All of us present had a long and, I believe, fruitful discussion about whether he was a political leader or a Nigerian elite. We concurred on the former.

The political system in Nigeria is highly skewed to the advantage of the well off and as the rake off is worthy of investing in for the political class, many people with nefarious past and no reasons at all to be considered for public office are seen jostling for same. The rake off or pay off is found to be juicy enough to necessitate killings, maiming and general violence by these unscrupulous political gladiators, thereby eliminating or discouraging participation by the more cerebral, serious and public-minded would-be politicians.

Violence based on desperation will always be an element as long as the remuneration is astronomically high and not commensurate with the job description or person specification. And this is clearly in evidence and the case with Nigerian elected politicians, especially in the National Assembly. Nigerian political post-holders and leaders are one of the best paid politicians in the world with nothing tangible to be shown for the betterment of the society as their output to justify the pay.

Ideally, there is no justification why an elected member of National house of Assembly (with or without requisite experience) should earn a take-home package that is more than that of a director-general in the civil service or a professor in the university sector. These are professionals who have spent decades honing their experience and know-how to be at the top of their game, as against most members of the National Assembly who ideally should be treated and accorded benefits worthy of an intern in any reputable organization worthy of its salt.

It may be argued that National Assembly members have constituency duties and services to perform, hence some additional expenses; however, one can equally argue that those constituency duties and services are shirked and not provided by majority of the members of National assembly, so it will generally not be missed by the constituents if not provided and hence, should not be allowed for in their remuneration at all.

Public services should not be an avenue to line ones pocket but an opportunity to serve ones community selflessly; and when in office, providing the vision of a better day ahead backed with policies and agendas to aid in getting to the better day. Nigerians politicians generally lack this ideal, hence, apathy amongst electorate in the past. However, Nigerian electorates are slowly waking up and any so-called and would-be political leaders should better wake up too and smell the coffee. It's definitely not java!

In normal societies, political leaders are serious public servants, but in Nigeria, the reverse is the case with the political post-holders acting as overlords and uncrowned princes of the Nigerian nation. They seek and get kick-backs for carrying out their constitutional duties as executives and as legislators, abuse the appropriation and oversight functions; use their positions to influence contract awards from MDAs; tamper with MDAs recruitment and promotion processes etc. etc.

Everything in Nigeria and the thinking of the leaders are upside down. In normal climes, political leaders strive to ensure that public services are provided and maintained to the required standard so that they are able to enjoy their personal time in peace and quiet with their family and loved ones. In Nigeria, the opposite suffice. Political leaders strive to ensure that public services does not work by looting the funds, so that they can play the benefactor to the public directly and get their adulation while the resulting hypertension and high blood pressure that comes with the associated stress are seen as signs of being a big man or woman. Foolish and ignorant lot!

A typical Nigerian leader sought adulation for works or projects he may have completed while in office with public funds. These are works or projects which form part of his or her core duties in office, and in any case, he or she is being paid salary for those duties. Of course, the Nigerian masses have their part to play in the self-obsession by their so-called leaders. The Nigerian people are always happy to accredit work, which in many climes will be the output of a normal day at work for any politician, to the magnanimity and generosity of the Nigerian politician.

It is pertinent to say at this juncture that the Nigerian leaders are apt and accurate reflection of the Nigerian people. What you see in an average Nigerian leader is what exists in the average mass on the street. It is common for a working class Nigerian to complain about the excesses of the average Nigerian leaders only to surpass the excesses him/herself on his/er own ascension into a leadership role overnight by election or otherwise.

Of course, there have been modest, responsible and community welfare-minded leaders in the history of Nigeria with enviable, notable and identifiable track record in the history of the potentially great nation. The likes of Nnamdi Azikiwe, Tafawa Balewa, Obafemi

Awolowo etc. come immediately to mind. However, the mould from which those crops of leaders were made has been broken and today's crops are of inferior, morally and intellectually deficient mould.

The few morally and intellectually upstanding responsible Nigerian leaders of today, in conjunction with the reasonable Nigerian masses, owe it to the generality of Nigerian people to ensure the sanitization of the leadership rank and file and set a strict criteria on ascension to a leadership role in the country at no exclusion of any individual based on socio-economic, political or ethno-religious basis. It is an uphill task considering the herd mentality of the average Nigerian.

The leadership reform, indeed, will have to be a top-down approach. Remuneration of elected officials will need to be aligned with the civil/public servant salary structure and all the irrelevant allowances discontinued. This remuneration reform, as a small gesture will help in a multi-faceted way by firstly making the elective post unattractive to carpetbaggers. Secondly, it will encourage individuals with genuine intentions to serve the public, without the obscene spending ability required right now, to venture into politics and vie to serve conscientiously on a level playing ground. Thirdly, it will reduce; if not totally eradicate big money and 'Godfatherism' in local politics and by extension, regional and national politics. The Presidency, the National Assembly, State Assemblies, RMAFC (Revenue mobilisation and fiscal commission etc.) all has a role to play, and of course, the masses have to lobby their representatives accordingly.

Elected political leaders are beginning to realize that with ever more transparent and tamper-proof elections in the country, they have to listen to their electorates and do their biddings to reclaim their mandate and remain relevant. This can only be good for Nigerian politics and public service delivery to the populace.

The Followers

The average Nigerian is impressionable and dogmatic in nature. They crave for the good things in life, yet are not willing or able to sacrifice the necessary inconveniences that are essential for incremental societal development.

Arguably, one cannot essentially distinguish the physiological and psychological state and make-up of leaders from that of the followers. An average Nigerian loathe the attitudes and exuberances of their leaders, yet they will descend to a much worse excesses ones they attain a relative ascendancy to leadership in their local groups, communities, regions, states or national level.

The average Nigerians does not realise that all good, developed and advanced nations and cities around the world were built by sweat, tears, pain and blood of their respective citizens at one time or the other. None was ever made what they are today by God or any divine power. Every Nigerian needs to come to the realisation that the extra wait on queues; going the extra mile than is necessary; the extra delay for following due process without bribing; the provision of adequate and making sure of timely service that one is being paid a salary for is dispensed judiciously; taking ownership and judicious care of public assets in one's care; ensuring public funds are used for its set purposes etc. etc. are all required to ensure a steady and incrementally advancing society with individual, communal and civic responsibilities dispensed without fear or favour.

The average Nigerian prays for god's intervention in the broken society that was deliberately broken by their peers or forefathers, failing to realise that what was broken by man can only be unbroken by man back. The dogmatic belief of Nigerians in the two main dominant Abrahamic religions (Christianity and Islam) is a hindrance in nation building rather than an applaudable asset.

Nigeria should be a fully secular state, religions separated distinctly from the state. If I was cajoled to rule, all religious activities will be banned from all state functions. Religious belief should be a thing of the mind and personal between the believer and his/er god. On this theme too, the prevailing attitude of spending 30minutes out of a 40minute-speech to acknowledge the presence of so-called 'VIPs' and unnecessary protocol at official functions will be outlawed with immediate effect. What a sickening rigmarole of nonsense! And some will even have the audacity to come out 'to stand on the existing protocol' to show their sense of brevity. What a people!

Nigerians generally are favour-seeking and will not on a good day say the truth to power. An average Nigerian will normally rather tell a leader or someone in a position of power what the leader wants to hear rather than the truth and let everything else go asunder as long as s/he gets his/er gratification.

It is cultural in Nigeria, and indeed Africa, for the younger ones to respect their elders (or leaders) irrespective of the facts. This culture, in my opinion is germane to the state of Nigerian, and indeed African, stunted development and advancement. Having aides, assistant and ministers who are unable to look into the eyes of their principal and tell him/er that s/he is wrong, is the reason why Nigerians still wallow in immeasurable depravity today. Some politicians indeed take on assistants and advisers not on the basis of providing professional advice but as political 'settlement' for prior support (usually for questionable and/or illegal services provided) in their ascendancy process.

I have always contended that age is not sacrosanct. A stupid young man will grow up to be a stupid middle aged man and eventually a stupid old man. Age has never been an automatic reservoir of intelligence. It may serve well as a reservoir of experience, but experience comes secondary in today's fast evolving world where history does not repeat itself as often to render experience a front contender as a leadership requirement. Nigerians ought to have realised that with the incessant recycling of the same old crop of leaders who have hardly added any value to the national life qualitatively, economically or socially.

Let us not discount the tenacity of an average Nigerian. Nigerians can be hard-working, resourceful and dogged in achieving their aim, either good or bad. An average Nigerian have the can-do attitude and believes in his or her invincibility to the extent that they believe they can walk between raindrops, so, most foreigners find it difficult to understand the under-achievement of the nation state.

However, the societal and religious beliefs that all credit is due to god meant credit is never given or acknowledged by individuals when credit is due. The fake modesty of always giving thanks to god and failing to acknowledge human abilities when it excels meant mediocrity and genius is not differentiated and celebrated as such.

That is why in Nigeria, excellence, perfection and qualitative work output has been relegated to the backburner in place of mediocrity and low-quality mass work output which may, in the short term, be more financially rewarding. For example, it is a common knowledge that good and quality building work output are more easily achievable with Togolese and Republic of Benin artisans and builders rather than Nigerian ones. This is a very bad indictment on the Nigerian societal value system where perfection and quality has been thrown out of the window in place of the numerical number of work that can be completed to gain the maximum financial gain. Seeking of undeserved financial gains by Nigerians is the Achilles heel of the historical zeal for excellence of the Nigeria of old and the cause of all Nigerian societal woes today.

Leaders are made and not born. There is also a saying that goes thus "...Some are born great, some acquire greatness and some have greatness entrusted to them, but the greatest of all is he who can truly stand up and say 'I have played my part...' ". Most Nigerians cannot truly stand up to say they have played their part in the nation building of the present day Nigeria. Yet, they disparage the country and its leaders (not that they do not need disparaging) day in day out and at every turn without any constructive ideas on how to make things better. They demolish what is being built for their own personal gain, break laws which were normally created to provide a level playing ground. For example, I have not been able to get my head around the following three scenarios below, out of many, which I was made to understand are very rampant in Nigeria amongst the followership:

a) Digging up and thereby destroying of newly resurfaced communal highways by roadside hawkers during the night, to ensure that traffic will slow down thereby enabling the hawkers to effectively market their wares better to motorists during the day.

b) Stealing of communal electrical distribution and installation cables for sale to make commercial cooking utensils and other artefacts; and all for personal gains while throwing their own community into unwarranted darkness.

c) Blowing of oil pipelines from oil wells to protest degradation of the oil-producing areas and in the process, causing oil leakages and seepages which further degrade the oil-producing land, water and air.

One cannot really understand why anyone will opt to shoot him/herself in the foot in other to put food into his/er mouth. These scenarios above show the selfish and shallow thinking of some Nigerians. These are serious economic sabotage which the law/lawmakers, its enforcement agents/executive and the judiciary should take seriously. One needs to acknowledge the presence of some Nigerians within the arms of government who are always in the wings to frustrate the best efforts of government and well-meaning Nigerians, because they benefit directly or indirectly from theses illegal and economic sabotage.

The followers are blamed by a school of thought to be a net contributor to the excesses of the leaders;

however, one cannot be definitive of what comes first, the egg or the chicken? A school of thought believes that the leadership is always under a lot of financial pressure from the followership to provide their day to day need. I can believe this to an extent as I have first-hand experience of a political friend trying to satisfy a minimum of 200people daily coming to his home and office with their myriad of problems from health to economic, deaths to births, celebration to bereavement etc. etc. This school of thought believes that the demand of the followership on the leadership necessitates the need for the leadership to acquire wealth (legal and illegal) relentlessly to satisfy the incessant demand.

Another opposing school of thought believes that the excessive remuneration and allowances of the political leaders is actually the impetus that encouraged the followership to seek their share of the national cake from the political leaders.

One cannot say what came first like the case of the chicken and the egg, however, if the source of the largess or the financial incentive to seek political post is removed, the leadership will have no funds to throw around and the followership will eventually realise that political leaders are not cash cows but normal public servants like a normal civil servants (not the so-called super civil servants).

Religious Beliefs & Spirituality

Nigerians are very religious but not godly. There are more religious clerics per head in Nigeria than any other country in the world. Hardly would you see a Nigerian urban street without a multitude of churches, mosques or other religious gathering points. A new trend is for the rich to build a mosque and chapel within their compound to ensure their express transition to heaven irrespective of their inequities on earth.

To be a pastor or a man of god in Nigeria is fashionable because it commands a lot of respect in the society, especially amongst the congregation and followers; and the associated worldly wealth that comes with the position has never hurt anybody in the past.

I was born a Christian and still proclaim my Christianity, but I have come to realise that religion is the opium of the poor. A concept used to subjugate the repressed from revolting since time immemorial, with the pie-in-the-sky heavenly reward promised in exchange for remaining meek and subservient in this world, while the religious and other sectorial leaders reap earthly rewards on a daily basis without holding out for the much touted heavenly reward.

This is why Nigerians that can hardly feed themselves and their family will ensure that their tithe of 10% does not go unpaid to churches that use the tithes to start commercial ventures like universities which the contributors of the tithes are unable to access for their own children and wards because of high and excessive fees.

Some Nigerians are indeed weird and sometimes seemingly senseless set of people.

Only in Nigeria will there be a need to set up a league of prayer warriors to pray for successful launch and completion of a project, where all that is needed is planning and resources (financial, material, equipment and manpower) – all within the remit of a mere mortal.

Nothing happens in Nigeria without a religious and spiritual angle attached to it. We have all heard of a former president that spent billions of Naira, the Nigerian currency, on Imams and Pastors to wage politically motivated praying war on his political opponents; but all to no avail as he was unseated in a most unfashionable and 'unNigerian' way.

Initially, I had always thought the spiritual manifestation in all things as a mind-set and way of thinking is restricted to the uneducated, poor and down-trodden section of the Nigerian society, but I have been amazed that the mind-set cuts across all sections of the society, from highly educated to the uneducated, from immensely rich to the very poor, from the elites to the down-trodden.

I have often discussed issues with more objective Nigerians and the conclusion that we have arrived at is that Nigerians have affinity to shirk their responsibilities and appropriate their failure to an imaginary unseen forces. That is why a Nigerian caught out in committing a criminal or immoral act will always blame it on the devil or the witches from his/er clan.

A Nigerian driver who knew all along that his tyres or brakes are on the blink and needed urgent change would manage it until a catastrophic event occurs; which he will then blame on the witches and wizards from his family or clan who are bent on him not becoming successful. I have always contended that most so-called 'accidents' on Nigerian roads (and other sectors) are not 'accidents' but foreseeable disasters caused by gross negligence and misconducts by the main actors who are responsible for those vehicle, machinery, equipment or infrastructure. For a mishap to be truly classified as an 'accident', it must be unforeseen and unpredictable. And where an unavoidable risk of occurrence is likely, it must be mitigated to reduce the probability of occurrence to the barest minimum. This is not the case in Nigeria, as health and safety in all endeavours is relegated to the backburner by successive legislative and executive arms of governments over the years.

I do not, as any reasonable Nigerian shouldn't, have any problem with anybody exercising their personal believes and spiritualism in their own space. I believe this is enshrined in the charter of human rights and universal freedom of an individual. Barging into my space is what I have issues with. If I want to, I should be able to attend a mosque or church of my choosing without having to apologise for it.

In the same trend, I will expect to enjoy the peace and quiet in my home without a church or mosque on mega loudspeakers espousing his or her beliefs into my home without seeking my consent in the first place. This is noise pollution and Nigerian governments (local, state and federal) needs to perform better in that aspect. Invariably, the non-separation of state and religion has hampered the ability of the legislative and executive arms of governments to perform their core responsibilities.

Compartmentalisation of religion and faith related issues as a personal issue and hence, between the faithful and his or her god is necessary to ensure that Nigeria as a nation utilise to the optimum, the easily achievable feats by we mere mortals. That clear separation is what has differentiated the achieving and successful nations of the world from the failing ones. If I was cajoled to rule, this separation will be cardinal.

Another absurd display of state involvement in religious issue is the organisation and sometime sponsorship of pilgrimage to Mecca and Jerusalem. I am unsure which government in Nigeria started the practice, but it was definitely a faux pas in all ramifications. It should be down to an individual to arrange his/er or passage for a pilgrimage for his/er own personal spiritual gain unless the state can make a case of communal benefit (which will mean the state at an institutional level acknowledging religion as a state sector) from the pilgrimage, which from where I am standing is not feasible nor provable.

Education of the masses or followership is inextricably important to nation building. By education, I do not mean the literacy and numeracy aspect alone, the education I have in mind centres mainly on critical thinking and ability to assimilate facts and separation of these facts from the 'alternative facts' being floated around. Inability to separate the truth from the 'alternative truth' is the bane of the failure of an average Nigerian. How can one explain the advice from a cleric to a faithful to blow him/herself up to enter heaven into the bosom of some 72 virgins, while the cleric himself is unwilling to enjoy these heavenly bounty but will rather grapple with the earthly tainted virgins. Yes, there are weak people that can be easily brainwashed, but the test of a good and responsible government is the ability to look after the weak, malleable-minded and down-trodden in its society; and not the ability to provide opportunities and wealth to the strong few at the expense of the overall society. If I was cajoled, the rich, which have invariably gained their wealth at the expense of the poor, will pay their fair share of socially helping the weak and the down-trodden to maintain a socially acceptable minimum standard level of living by way of progressive taxation.

The average Nigerian is not able to differentiate real and fake news. The media and other revered institutions also perpetuate the trend of publishing unverified news items as real. Terrestrial and satellite televisions and radio are rampant with dramas perpetuating fake spiritual and religious stories which the larger portion of the populace takes in hook, line and sinker as the gospel truth. A stringent code of conduct and practice needs to be negotiated or voluntarily self-imposed by the media industry. Mostly, the quality of programmes, news and investigative reporting at present is poor and unprofessional.

My opinion, as a Nigerian, is quite tangential to the global religious mainstream beliefs of fervent believers of the two main religions in Nigeria i.e. Islam and Christianity.

Although both religions are foreign to Africa, Nigerians and other Africans, being what they are, believe they now know the Gods of the two religions more than the colonialists who introduced the religions to them. Only in Africa, especially Nigeria, did the local population jettison their own local beliefs and religion in place of the foreign religions introduced by the colonising power. It was never the case in Asia e.g. China, India, Singapore, Malaysia etc. that the locals abandoned their local religious beliefs in place of the colonialists'; just as slave trade was never practiced on a global scale in any other continent colonised around the world apart from Africa. Africans are still wallowing in self-denial, low self-esteem and inferiority complex that fed the many injustices visited upon them.

The God/s of these religions are said to be all powerful, omnipresent and omnipotent. He doesn't and wouldn't need services of the mortal charlatans, idiots and religious bigots masquerading themselves as self-appointed religious warriors to kill and maim in his name. He is in a, much more, better position to wage his own wars against non-believers or aggressors as he deem fit. Since humans created God in their own likeness, they have ever so much ascribed human characteristics to God and those who have realised have, for ever and ever, taken advantage of the reverence of believers to exploit them; nowhere more so than within the present day Nigerian societies, home and away.

Mind-set and Traditional/Cultural Beliefs

The followership in Nigeria is seen as gullible by the leadership, or how else can one rationalise Nigerian politicians using ethnicity and religion to divide and rule. Lack of education may be a contributing factor but if people are able to be street-wise without formal education, why not be situation-wise too. The Nigerian masses need to sit up and prove the leadership wrong by refusing to be mobilised on the basis of ethnicity or religion, but by facts, figures and ability to deliver on communal expectations and yearnings.

The common enemy of an average Nigerian, irrespective of their religion or ethnicity, are not their opposite numbers from other religions and ethnic groups; but they are the political leaders across the board who exploit them socially, economically and materially. The leaders use ethnicity and/or religion to ensure their own relevance in national politics and to achieve their own selfish ambitions.

Ethnicity, and indeed geographical situation or location, is an accident of birth because all were created equal. Religion is an acquired taste due to the accident of birth. No man or woman chooses both from birth and no man or woman should have to or be required to defend or fight or agitate what was, what is and what will be after his or her demise.

Nigerians with their uninhibited appetite for foreign religions are also rooted in their traditional, superstitious and cultural beliefs, hence, the dichotomy and split personalities usually displayed by the average Nigerian. Arguably, if god exists, then so must the devil. There is no good without evil. So, invariably, if the god of the foreign Abrahamic religions is good, the local gods of the local traditional beliefs must be evil. That is the logic of the average Nigerian adoptee of these foreign religions.

An average Nigerian believes in superstitions more than facts staring them in the eye. How can you, rationalise an adult and reasonable sane man believing that using human parts in rituals can successfully make him/er rich. I had always jested with believers of the existence of the money ritual that I wonder where their perceived spirit buys his/er minting press and paper from, or whether the money disappears from CBN(central Bank of Nigeria) without them having the inkling of the spiritually inspired currency disappearing act.

These superstitious beliefs are inbred in every Nigerian from birth and only those who make conscious effort to rid themselves of this mind-set ever see the evil, damage and regression that these beliefs have caused Nigeria as a nation and black Africa continentally. The beliefs are not restricted to the

Nigerians within Nigeria alone, it manifests in most Nigerians and Africans in the diaspora too.

The true evil that exists in Nigeria are those political leaders and their puppeteers who milk the country dry and fail to realise that social coherence and security or insecurity will translate to their own security or insecurity too. And believe me; they are as mortal as you and me but greedy than a herd of swine.

The leadership and followership as a combined people of the Nigerian nation are not sincere and principled in their acts to themselves or one another.

Nigerians will invoke or demand the 'all-embracing loyalty or allegiance' from their friends, allies, acquaintances, families and dependants etc. to seek support whenever they have done something wrong or about to do something wrong. And usually, depending on the reliance of these people, or not, on the loyalty-invoker, they oblige or welch. Often than not, a Nigerian will oblige rather than welch because of the unforeseen but possible benefits that may accrue from such obligation (even at the detriment to the loyalist's immediate community); thereby perpetuating the vicious cycle of sustaining corruption or any other nefarious acts that the loyalty invoker may have committed or about to commit.

The quintessential Nigerians were altruistic and community-focused, however, the new breed of Nigerians are individualistic, self-obsessed and self-seeking. Something went wrong along the line and it is a terrible indictment of the Nigerian leadership primarily, and of course, with the followership closely in tow.

Nigerians(leadership and followership) come across as being confident and savvy consumers, but their consumptive appetite is mainly based and fired up because of their lack of self-confidence and inferiority complex to everything foreign.

An average Nigerian believes that by wearing a foreign expensive 'mass produced' designer label makes them superior to their fellow Nigerians. It makes them feel special and unique wearing a clothing-label that churns out thousands or millions of products a year, or even daily.

It always amazes the way some Nigerians espouse and gloat over worldly luxury possession like jewelleries, cars etc. which makes them feel in a class of their own while forgetting that some innovative and well-grounded individuals unlike them built the brands and manufactures the product or renders the service. Mostly, these services and products are provided to millions of people around the globe annually, hardly making the object of their presumed superiority unique or outstanding.

The wrong Nigerian mentality of believing that self-worthiness and achievement is based on the quantity and quality of what one consumes rather than the quantity and quality of what one produces is what makes the clear-day difference between the developed and economic powerhouses like China, UK, the US etc. on the one hand, and developing nations like Nigeria and others, on the other.

Of course, it is automatic that once you concentrate on production of good quality products and services in-country, increase in local consumption of these good quality products and services is a natural progression and it will become pervading and more easily accessible to a greater majority, thereby lifting the general living condition and lifestyle of the local people, and the economic wellbeing of the nation; such as it now exists amongst the Asian tiger nations. A contemporary example is China. Whether Nigeria, and indeed other African nations that represents the majority of developing nations, has the focus, dedication and tenacity to achieve the same feat is yet to be seen.

The niche products and services market, for those who have worked hard for their money and crave the exclusivity that their rightfully gained wealth can buy, will always be there, but ideally it should not be from wrongfully gained wealth or from public-purse pilfering and lootings as the case subsist in Nigeria.

Diligence and hard work are an accomplishing combination that has slowly crept out of the lexicon of majority of Nigerians (and indeed many Africans), hence, the overly reliance on miracles, spiritual interventions and beliefs in other unsavoury practices for survival. While other races in other climes in the world have their beliefs, but rely and are successfully using research and development in science and technology to find solutions to their immediate problems and define the future that we will all have to live in.

Nigeria is where you will see a football team that has not put enough effort into practice go to a pastor or herbalist to ask for spiritual intervention to win a match; a student that had failed to study hard go to herbalist or pastor for spiritual intervention or buy a miracle pen that will aid in passing an exam; a job-seeker seeking spiritual intervention to get a job that he is neither qualified nor able to perform etc. etc. The list is unlimited and the range is as wide as human endeavour endures.

Entrepreneurial Nigerians seeing the opportunities of fleecing the millions of gullible Nigerians have set up shop as pastors, imams or herbalist to provide the pie-in-the-sky service that these gullible Nigerians sought. Government should have a regulatory and registration regime for the practitioners in these sectors to differentiate the charlatans from the professionals providing real and feasible service that is fit for purpose.

It is debatable to what extent the spiritual service providers (including the pastors and imams) are helpful or damaging to the country. I see them as alternative psychotherapists whose services can be very useful for calming and taming the neurotics and psychologically strained and damaged Nigerians. They counsel, advocate, advice and if all that fails, they will also promise their believers that they will intervene on their behalf on the spiritual level. You can't beat that! And in a country of about one qualified psychotherapist to about tens of thousands of people, the spiritual service providers offer a lot of self-help. In the same vain, as most are charlatans in the business to make money, they prey on the gullible by spreading fear, anxiety and paranoia to ensure their clientele parts away with the content of their wallet in very extraordinary ways. These are the original 419ers! The progenitors of today's 419ers!

If one is to be truthful and evaluate the psychiatric state and make-up of an average Nigerian mind, the symptomatic hallmarks of delusional psychosis is apparent and more than usual, often present. Historically, under Karl Jaspers classification of psychotic delusions into primary and secondary delusions, an average Nigerian suffers from secondary delusion which is known and identified to be influenced by the person's background or current situation such as ethnicity, religion, political, superstitions and other cognitive beliefs. Unlike the primary delusion which arises suddenly without any mental process comprehensibility.

Delusion is commonly defined as an unrelenting sense of certainty maintained despite strong contradictory evidence. Hence, an average Nigerian believes that some entity (usually on a spiritual level) is always attempting to harm or derail them when obvious contradictory prove exists (persecutory delusion) or in the 'delusion of grandiosity' which is common amongst the Nigerian political and religious leaders, whereby one believes he or she possesses some special power or influences beyond ones actual limits.

Other psychotic delusional types common amongst Nigerians will include delusion of reference (where an aspect of one's experience is referenced as being a message or act from an external influencing entity), thoughts insertion (where ones thought is believed to be inserted by an external entity or not one's own thought) and thoughts broadcasting (where ones thought is believed to be audible and broadcasted to the whole world or the people in the vicinity).

Nigerians are seen as undisciplined and ungovernable by successive Nigeria governments, however, most government fail to understand the root of the problem as the endemic corruption that has pervaded every fabric of the society at all levels.

Nigerians can be as law-abiding as the next man and as disciplined as a monk in keeping his vows, if the law of the land is followed to the letter and erring individuals are punished as stipulated by the existing laws without fear or favour. There may exist a little bit of attitudinal divergence in money crimes committed by Nigerians in diaspora. The incentives associated with living large and being able to 'oppress' in Nigeria, and indeed in diaspora, relegates the normal sense of self-preservation of an average Nigerian to take the risks of incarceration and penalties associated with their crimes to the backburner. Of course, these pockets of hard-core and persistent law-breakers exist in every community of every nation on every continent in the world.

I have known and experienced Nigerians being rowdy at their point of departure in Nigeria and being as orderly as a group of sisters awaiting the holy sacrament at their point of arrival outside the shores of Nigeria. What can be responsible for the change? What is obvious is that the fear of facing the wrath of the law in the foreign country and the inability to influence the course of the law enforcement process is a main factor.

So, in all ramifications, the inability of the Nigerian police force, the primary law enforcement agency, to judiciously enforce the law of the land, without prejudice or malice, has a major impact on the indiscipline and lawlessness of Nigerians. No new laws are needed in Nigeria as all the laws presently on the statute book are adequate when properly enforced judiciously across the board.

Presently, the Nigerian police force is one of the most corrupt government's agencies in Nigeria and needs urgent purging of corrupt officers and an all-encompassing reform that should ideally be on a clean sheet.

An average Nigerian is corrupt by nature and expects the other Nigerians that s/he interfaces with to be as corrupt too. Hence, even when bribes or inducement are not requested, they are offered. Even when bribe is not in demand, a Nigerian will offer bribe to gain advantage over assumed competitors, adversaries and rivals. It is very difficult and almost impossible not to be corrupt in Nigeria as you see advantages skewed to favour bribers at every turn. You see corruption at all levels and it affects you daily at work, home or play.

Corruption, as rightly identified by the present government in Nigeria, is the most damaging force that is debilitating to achieving any meaningful social and economic advancement in Nigeria.

Most Nigerians will identify corruption as the most entrenched and damaging practice in Nigeria, and if they were asked further and truthful in their response, they will also concede that they themselves perpetuate corruption in one or more of its variant forms at least four to five times or even more daily. Simply, it is a way of life that needs to be heavily combated without taking any options off the table in the war against it.

CHAPTER TWO -Current National Challenges

Size & Structure of Government

The size and structure of the Nigerian federation has been on the front burner for many different reasons in recent times. My view is quite simple. As the acronym and cliché goes 'KISS – keep it short/straight and simple'.

I am not going to be popular with the civil servants, current and would-be, and the various labour unions representing their single-issue agendas. Luckily, I don't hope to seek votes from these constituencies since I hope to be cajoled to rule.

The civil service at all levels (federal, state and local) are simply over-bloated and does not in any way represent value for money, and as long as Nigerian political leaders sees the civil service as a social service for their loyal supporters and political allies, the civil service will always be a source of drain and perpetual leakage on the public finances.

The civil service ideally does not provide any tangible goods or service which contributes to the gross domestic product (GDP) of the country, yet it consumes around 60% of the annual budget of the country. In as much as, by number, it represents less than 20% of the overall population of the country.

The civil service should ideally be restricted to formulation, implementation and monitoring of policies for all sectors of the economy; these in my view are the core function of the civil service and government. All other non-core activities, especially commercial activities etc., carried out presently by the government should either be outsourced to the private sector or left to the private sector to be provided on a competitive and commercial market terms and rates (or subsidised if necessary).

It is a common knowledge that the private sector is the driver of growth in an economy and a vibrant and robust private sector ensures low unemployment rate which is a major factor for an economically and upwardly mobile society. High unemployment rate is the underlying cause of most of the youth restlessness and ills in the society and across Nigeria at the moment.

I am an unashamed advocate of a wholesome privatisation and commercialisation of all sectors of the economy with a policy framework provided by government to ensure quality of goods and services with a guarantee of a level playing ground for all the players in the market. If this approach is embraced, the number and quality of civil servants needed, and hence employed, will be drastically changed to a manageable, effective and efficient number.

Despite the long term of government being in business a public sector player, they still lack the learning curves achieved by the private sector; and the effectiveness and efficiency thereof.

I do not see any MDAs of government which cannot be privatised wholly (apart from the policy formulation, implementation and monitoring units) or partially. Even, the so-called free public services etc. can be privatised as long as they are free at the point of delivery to the members of the public at a private sector efficiency level.

The federal structure of the government is flawed in concept for a country of over 923,000 square kilometre land area and over 180 million people. Over-centralisation of power in the middle is an aberration of a federal system.

For example, it is absurd for FERMA located majorly in Abuja to want to oversee the maintenance of federal roads throughout the nooks and crannies of the country. Ideally, federal government should concentrate on big-ticket major inter-regional/states road constructions and infrastructures procured with the private sector and on completion, hand it over to be adopted by resident states for the whole life cycle maintenance of the infrastructure. The section of a cross-country or regional road that falls into the jurisdiction of a state who fails to adopt the section or fails to maintain adopted roads to required standard may be privatized and tolled accordingly for maintenance up to the required standard. The elected leaders of such states will now have to answer to their electorates why the section of the road in the state is tolled while others are not.

The argument of what structure the Nigerian federation should adopt is neither here or there. I am of the school of thought that Nigeria should jettison the adoption of any foreign system of government and develop an home-grown system that is suitable, cheap and workable in Nigeria's peculiar environment. However, working with what we have now, I am of the opinion that a fully blown out three-tier government is not necessarily prudent, effective, efficient nor useful. I will propose a slimmed down two-tier system with less power in the centre (or federal level) and a more robust and powerful local government being the closest to the people and their day to day life. The local governments may come with the option of collaborating with other local governments to form a region and pool resources together to achieve economy of scale and uniformity in infrastructural development and industrialisation.

Public Salary Structure

The disparity in public salary structure needs to be harmonised from the current situation where different service commissions having different pay scales.

All public servants (civil servants, politically elected, political appointees etc.), whether federal, state or local government should be on a harmonised public salary structure that is defined and applicable across the board. The pay may however be weighted based on local cost of living allowances.

In my view, a reasonable guide will be that the highest paid public servant on this harmonised salary structure should not ideally earn more than 10 times the amount earned by the lowest public servant on the salary structure (subject to local weighting) i.e. if the lowest take-home salary is N36, 000/month then the highest take-home salary on the structure (within the same weighting locality) should not exceed N360, 000/month. This will ensure a transparent structure and invariably discourage charlatans coming into public service for nefarious reasons.

Poor Service Level in Public Organizations

It is always amazing to see the slow grinding as the wheel of government machinery turns slowly, almost painfully, because there are no set goals and targets to achieve.

Most decisions to be taken at all levels of government majorly are restricted to three outcomes after scrutiny – Agree, Not Agree or Incomplete. So, it amazes me that processes are stalled and files are kept in the system for months without any reasons at all except as leverage to seek bribe from benefitting party of the decision on the file.

If I was cajoled to rule, service level agreements (SLAs) will be the order of the day and all MDAs will enter into SLAs with all other MDAs that use the work output of their units, and also enter a similar SLA on services provided to the members of the public at large. For example, signing-off of a verified and authorised contractual certificate of payment to a contractor should be done within 24hrs. Any officer that fails to meet the terms of a SLA without a cogent reason will invariably have to face the music and dance 'palongo' (a crazy Nigerian dance step) to the music. Public servants need to buckle up. They must represent value for money and must be fit for the purpose for which they were engaged.

As every other thing in Nigeria, monitoring/enforcement to achieve a set standard seem to be the main and underlying problem. Those set standards are always there but there is always a disconnection between policy formulation, implementation and monitoring or enforcement. In addition to implementation of SLAs, key performance indicators (KPIs) should also be developed as a metric to measure the level of performance of various MDAs against indicators of key areas of the core duties of the MDAs.

Constituency Projects

The aberration and now a standard practice of the legislature to budget and claim a project annually per legislator as their constituency project is one of the reasons why Nigerians abhor all that the legislature represents in all ramification.

Project execution and prioritisation should be the exclusive right of the executive according to the nation's needs and should not be secured and used as a leveraging and bargaining tool for the return of a legislator back to the legislature during elections.

Indeed, if there are constituency requirements, the legislators are tasked and voted for in the first place to bring the attention of the executive to such requirements but not in the way constituency projects has been turned into questionable and unsustainable empowerment programmes for boosting the popularity of legislators in their respective constituency by doling out of tricycles, motorcycles, sewing machines etc. which are usually sold out by mostly unworthy recipients who are usually chosen based on loyalty to the legislator.

Financial and Electoral Independence of Local Governments

The financial and electoral dependence on the states by local government runs roughshod against the tenets of the independent three-tier governance that Nigeria strives to achieve.

The Nigeria Financial Intelligence Unit (NFIU) has, to a certain degree, tried to stem the financial dependency; however, the dependence on the whims of state governors to carry out local government elections is still a political misalignment that needs to be tackled legislatively by the National Assembly.

I do not see the sensibility in a state governor that wants to embrace the duties of the local government when he is yet to excel in his own statutory duties of performing the responsibilities entrusted to him/er as the state governor.

The particular encroachment into the local government sphere of operation by state governors is cantankerous and disruptive to the governance at local governments across the nation. The operation of the unconstitutional Nigerian Governor's Forum (NGF) meant these illegal acts of the governors are replicated in most of the states of the federation flagrantly, apart from few, and tolerated by the federal executive arm and legislature to the chagrin of Nigerians.

The constitution itself is faulty in the replication of the Independent National Electoral Body in all states and the choice of the chairman of the state's electoral board being entrusted to the sitting state governor. This has meant the governors' deciding and entrusting the local governments to caretaker chairmen as opposed to the elected chairmen; only to have elections when they have consolidated power to the extent that they can manipulate and ensure the election of their stooges as their elected chairmen across the state's network of local governments.

It is a travesty, a pure and blatant abuse of the democratic process which is endorsed and legalized only in Nigeria. The country only requires the federal Independent National Electoral Commission (INEC) who carries out all the federal and states electoral processes to extend it services to the local government tier as well. No one has been able to postulate any reasonable justification for setting up Independent State Electoral Commission as it exists to carry out just the local government elections.

The monthly financial allocation paid via the states to the local governments also calls for concern and one needs to wonder why it can be so under any circumstances, unless the drafters of the constitution are biased one way or the other; or hadn't foreseen the undue advantage that it will give the governors in interfering with local government governance because of wielding such overwhelming financial control.

Abuse of charity status by faith groups

I am not known to be too religious, yet, known to respect individual's freedom to be as religious as they want as long as it doesn't infringe on their neighbour's rights. I've always been a believer of the cliché that your right stops where mine begins. So, in that respect, I think the religious groups in Nigeria are really taking the biscuit and the government are allowing them to get away with it.

How else can you explain a religious body under its charity status carrying out commercial ventures to the extent that it is on par or even more profitable than a wholly commercial venture, and yet exempted from paying tax?

In my view, the charity status that all religious body enjoys should be stripped-off and their religious operation should be taxable, albeit at a subsidized rate based on the amount of true charitable work that they do in the society, and their commercial ventures taxed as a wholly commercial venture at the going tax rate of the day for commercial ventures.

It is not too much to expect the religious bodies and organisations to provide qualitative and quantitative education and/or other social services free-of-any-charge to the people as charitable organisations, instead what we see are these charitable organisations charging exorbitant fees at their education facilities, fees at which most of their congregation who created the wealth of these charitable organisations are unable to afford for their children.

These days, religious bodies and organisations are into the very lucrative private education sector, water bottling, bread-making etc. As all things in Nigeria, the requirement for experience, technical or technological knowhow and core-competence in a venture are no barriers to enter and operate in any field of choice as long as you have deep pocket and very obedient and dogmatic followers who will buy into whatever your venture spills out hook, line and sinker. Overall, there is nothing wrong in using what you have to get what you want, same as just 'giving unto Caesar what is Caesar's'.

Religious bodies should simply pay taxes as any earthly body and wait to get their tax refunds in heaven!

Herdsmen/Farmers Clashes

This issue seems to be a very emotive topic for the two contending forces in the clashes. I will try as much as possible to be clinical and use logic by discarding any sentimental and emotional arguments put forward by any of the contending forces.

Cattle rearing are not different from any other form of animal husbandry; and it will be stupid to see and try to make any argument about its uniqueness or difference.

What we have to contend on is whether animals are reared to replace humans or are animals are reared to sustain human beings? In my mind of minds, animals are reared to sustain humans and not the other way round.

The advocacy of cattle ranches, in my opinion, is the way forward, albeit, as a private sector driven concern. I think the proposed involvement of the government in acquisition of ranches for cattle rearing is erroneous and sets a precipitous precedent that may come back to haunt the government.

Like all other private sector animal husbandry and poultry businesses that incur costs on their inputs like animal feed and veterinary costs, why do cattle herders want to skip out on input costs incurred by others by feeding their cattle for free, bedding them for free etc. Cattle rearing are businesses and must be treated as such. It must not and cannot be seen to enjoy any state subvention that will be discriminatory against all other animal husbandry businesses like commercial rearing of goats, sheep, poultry, pigs etc. in the country.

In actual fact, in a case for food hygiene, health and safety for humans, a passport system needs to be developed for all animals coming into the food chain to ensure proper records like vaccination, age, breed etc. can be accessed before entering the food chain. Cattle, as other animals reared for human consumption, needs to be monitored from birth to the abattoir, thus, an additional case for ranching as the most reliable way of knowing the quality and source of the meat that Nigerians put on their tables.

Tradition is dynamic and a progressive society is one that adopts and embraces changes that will be efficient, effective, alleviate the conditions and lifestyle of their people and animals. A retrogressive society, on the other hand, holds on nostalgically to old traditions which will make them uncompetitive and economically unsustainable until they become irrelevant or actually extinct. Nomadic cattle's rearing is archaic and should be called what it is!

Beggar's Mentality and Demeanour

If you were potentially rich and talented but in bondage for a number of years, you can be forgiven for not achieving your potentials; however, on being released from your bondage and being freed to use your talent to actualise your potential wealth and greatness, failure to achieve a quantum level of success is unforgivable.

It is disheartening to see the same person go back, cap in hand, begging those who had put him/er in bondage for several years, with a leaky cap in hand, asking for hand-outs again. It is simply defeatist and not a winning attitude, it is a subservient and slavery mentality that has never been any good nor adopted by successful nations throughout history.

The penchant of African governments, and indeed Nigerian government, to seek unfavourable grants, loans, subsidies etc. from various foreign governments should be an embarrassment to the continent.

Apart from loans, and I mean favourable and reasonable loans, which are needed for outright development, industrialisation and economic growth, Nigeria should evaluate more closely the quality of subsidies, grants and loans that it obtains.

There is no free lunch anywhere and if you decide to get a loan for the lunch, you must not accept a condition whereby the lender dictates what you eat and where you must dine. You will definitely be short changed and you will still end up paying the loan and interest back.

Infrastructural loans whereby lender dictates or insists on their home grown deliverer (i.e. contractors) cannot be good for the debtor and had never been value-for-money anywhere in the world. What happened to good old competitive tendering and other competitive variants?

The Chinese loans currently in vogue in Nigerian infrastructural development, while it looks good on the surface, is the classical form of round-tripping whereby, for example, you are given a loan of US$1000.00 for 1year, at say a single-digit interest rate of 5% or less, to construct an Infrastructure barely worth US$700.00. You are then required to use a Chinese (Design & Build) contractor, consultants etc. who will charge you the full US$1000.00 for the completed infrastructure.

All professionals on the project will be expatriates from China with Nigerians employed as menial workers and fewer as professionals. The total wage bill paid to all workers on the project will be about US$200 with about US$50 of the US$200 paid to the Nigerian professionals and menial workers. US$300 goes towards plants, machinery and materials.

The remaining portion of the loan (US$500) goes towards the profit of the Chinese company and government (and of course, bribing of a stupid Nigeria who is ready to sell out his country). Overall, what Nigeria gets out of the deal is US$700 worth of infrastructure and employment of its teeming unemployed youths to the tune of just US$50. No technological transfer nor is there any form of advancement in the experience curve achieved by Nigerians on the project.

The Chinese on the other hand, apart from the immediate financial gains by the Chinese company and government from the capital and interest repayments, gets their local industries working full time to supply all the plants and machineries, and almost all the materials thereby keeping all related Chinese industries in production and keeping their employment rate relatively high and their economy healthy.

Where Nigeria and most Africans fail to realise is that experience is the best teacher; and that slow and steady has always been a good recipe for winning the race and I'm not saying we should re-invent the wheel. The only instance to go foreign is when you need to go fast and steady but you lack local technical know-how to effect the necessary quick changes. In such situations, it's always the best thing to go for the most advanced infrastructure available and ensure technological and knowledge transfer in the process. For example, why go for old technology like the diesel-fired train system when there are high-speed electric trains out there. One would think that Nigeria with its power-outage problems cannot sustain an electric-powered train network, but one or two dedicated power generation plants will provide enough juice to power a more comprehensive network than is being constructed now and it will be clean and future-proof for a time.

Nigeria has qualified engineers and other built environment professionals doing great things around the world and in Nigeria. The downside is that the Nigerian government by over-reliance on foreign contractors stifle the continuous professional development of both the home-based and diaspora professionals. Though, it can be said in support of the government that the Nigerian professionals' attitude, work ethics, competence, professionalism and moral conduct can be found wanting. Even diaspora Nigeria professionals, who have been exposed to stricter work ethics and high level of professionalism in their abode, soon revert back to type and the Nigerian way of doing things within a twinkle of an eye on exposure to the flawed system in Nigeria. It's almost like swimming against the tide, so they just give up and flow with the tide.

Dependence of African national governments on grants, subsidies etc. from NGOs, not-for profit organisations and charities whilst the continent is endowed with almost 50% of all natural resources on the globe is pathetic and should candidly be embarrassing to the purported leaderships of the continent.

Collectively the leadership have failed their respective countries and psyche.

Exclusion by Non-Taxation

Nigeria is one of the few nations in the world where personal taxation is not made compulsory or enforced amongst the unstructured workforce. At the advent of the oil discovery, the then government slowly disregarded revenue stream coming from taxation of the people in place of the immense foreign revenue from oil sales. Some will contend that it was a ploy by the government to disengage the populace from requesting for accountability of the tax collected from them. If that was the case, it worked.

An average Nigerian sees the government as a separate entity from the populace and it reflects on why the people do not take ownership of government-sponsored programs, infrastructures and properties. In my humble opinion, I believe the apathy by the populace contributed to the non-accountability by the leaders and the extraordinary level of corruption in the government.

It will be difficult for a political leader to dip his/er hand in the public kitty when s/he knows that all eyes are on him/er on how the tax collected from the populace is spent. Conversely, the populace will request for more accountability and will definitely not agree to the obnoxious and excessive remuneration that Nigeria political leaders currently enjoy and pay themselves.

Whilst the Nigerian government and its oil industry arm, NNPC ensures that the populace are in the dark as to the exact amount of money made from oil as a nation, the populace are not in any way concerned about the revenue receipt by the federal government. If anything, they see any government sponsored socio-economic and developmental projects as solely a government project for the people because of the government's magnanimity.

If anything, all working adults must be included in the tax net to ensure the inclusion of every voting adult in the decision on who to choose to run the country, what they are paid for the job and the level of accountability required from them to show that the taxpayers' monies are well spent.

Population Explosion

I have always been opposed to uninhibited growth of population in Nigeria or anywhere in the world. Of course, humans in government think in terms of economic value that a big population represents in terms of market size, value and available human resources to grow the economy. However, population explosion with a finite resources to sustain it is suicidal and recipe for implosion of the globe as we know it. As a former Nigerian president once said that population growth in Africa is a ticking time bomb for the continent. I will go a step further and say uninhibited population growth anywhere in the world is a ticking time bomb for the whole world.

The world has a finite reservoir of resources which can sustain life, most of which are non-renewables and are fast being used up by humans; and some renewables are being consumed at an unsustainable rate too. Of course, the earth has a self-healing and regulatory process in form of natural disasters and phenomenon which sometimes are triggered as the reactions to excessive human activities. Whilst these disasters sometimes wipe out thousands of humans in the space of few minutes or hours, human growth has steadily increased over the last few decades and bound to increase exponentially in the near future.

In Nigeria, I think the effects of uninhibited population explosion is already being felt from the conflicts between the herdsmen and farmers to the herds of uneducated, unemployed youth and Almajiris around the country. Scarce and unfairly distributed economic resources have resulted in human crimes such as kidnapping, robbery and generally brigandage across the length and breadth of the country.

My view is that Nigeria government may need, at a point, adopt a policy of childbirth-capping per person, couple or family unit. It would have been preferable if education and advocacy interventions can be enhanced to effect an attitudinal change in the average Nigerian, but I suspect the root of the traditional and religious beliefs are too deep to be uprooted and re-planted with more reasonable and logical outlook. Although population is projected to decrease in the west because of aging population, a boom is still projected for Asia and Africa to sustain the upward trend of global population.

In any case, the UN and all nations will have to come together to ensure a strategy for global population reduction or stabilisation, because unilateral decision taken by individual countries will not be effective with the globe that is fast becoming smaller and smaller with humans' vermin-like population explosion.

High Rate of Unemployment

The high rate of unemployment in Nigeria cannot at this point be blamed on population growth only. Actually at this point, the population is an asset which could have been properly harnessed and managed much more effectively and efficiently.

Most Nigerian youth complain of lack of employment, but if truth should be said, most of the youths are not well educated, employable, focused and result-oriented. It is a shame that the value of excellence and qualitative work has been eroded generally within the Nigerian ethos as explained in the next sub-heading.

The government of the day has now finally realized the error of over-relying on low-labour oil-production as the mainstay of the Nigerian economy. It is imperative that the economy is diversified and the private sector, which is regarded in every developed nation of the world as the engine-room of economic activities and growth, is allowed to play a very critical role, albeit with stringent regulatory regime by the government.

Nigerian youths with the support of the government, in terms of training and finance, must be encouraged to embrace the psyche of a job provider instead of a job seeker.

Corruption and the Yahoo Yahoo Phenomenon

The exposure of the level of rot and corruption within previous governments in Nigeria by the present government's war on corruption is unprecedented.

One feels ashamed to be associated with a country with so much filth and readiness of some so-called leaders to sometime embrace and hug the filth or justify the existence of the filth without any morsel of remorse.

Corruption has been an insidious and fettering vice that slipped into the Nigerian system over the years and has since become acceptable and sometimes glamourized in some circles.

Corruption is celebrated; as the source of people's wealth has become irrelevant and just being wealthy or rich is enough to pass the acceptability sniff test.

Mosques and churches, that are supposed to be the moral consciences of the nation, revere and celebrate the wealthy men and women with unknown or dodgy sources of income as long as they are able to write a big cheque for their religious house or organisation.

Fathers and mothers who are supposed to be the morality guardians of the family units have made corruption the foundation that the family morality is built on. It is not uncommon for parents to 'settle' (bribe) to ensure their wards are successful in gaining admissions to educational institutions. And of course, these inadequately prepared wards are unable to cope and survive through the educational rigours of the institutions; hence, they will resort to 'settlement' throughout their study and end up being an incompetent and unemployable graduate. This is the story of over 50% of Nigerian graduates today.

The leaders, especially political and religious ones, are very good at pointing fingers at the youths for their 'Yahoo Yahoo' or '419' escapades and the embarrassment of the nation in the process, while failing to admit that they were themselves the grand-daddies of 'Yahoo Yahooers' and '419ers'. They nurtured the youths.

I don't understand why it is hard for political and religious leaders to fathom the fact that the youth are only a reflection of the leaders and the society which bred, nurtured and influenced their characters.

Every sane and reasonable Nigerians, both within and without, feel ever so embarrassed about the childish and maniacal greed of the average Nigerian political (and indeed religious) leaders which has resulted in the under-development of the nation with failure in every human development indices. If we can be candid, the actions of the 419ers and Yahoo Yahooers are not quite different from that of the leaders (religious and political); the only difference being in their targeted victims only.

It is expected that a given percentage of any population will be negatively deviant, turn out to be real bad and/or display a certain degree of anti-social behaviour that the majority of the population will find appalling, that translates to a higher figure as the population increases, hence, with Nigeria's projected 200million population, that will be a hefty number.

All in all, Nigerians cannot be seen to be all bad; however, the concentration of Nigerian baddies in money-related crimes is astounding compared to any nation with similar population. The escapades of these bad eggs have overshadowed the brilliance and excellence of other professional law-abiding Nigerians who are doing great things in their chosen professional fields globally. So, it is not usually acknowledged and hence, it's surprising to note that the number of high-achieving Nigerian professionals around the globe far exceeds the average percentage of that expected in any similar population around the world with similar socio-economic and educational deprivations.

There used to be a time in my youth when nobody or parents wants to associate with people with unknown or dodgy sources of income or have their children play with their kids. The depth of moral decadence now meant that even moral defenders are willing to look the other way and celebrate these people with nefarious means of income. Actually, they want to associate with them as money defines success in Nigeria of today. Excellence, brilliance and achievements in chosen professional and productive fields are disregarded as long as the financial reward is not as palatable as that reckoned to indicate success. It is such a shallow way to think, yet this has become the mainstay view in the average Nigerian mind and that of the leaders, of course.

Simply, wealth of unknown source needs to be made unfashionable and deplorable again.

The way out for Nigeria is for the coalition of the sane and reasonable to mobilise and participate more in politics to politically wrestle the governance of the country from the current charlatans and carpetbaggers. The leaders give the country a bad stink and have destroyed the current Nigerian youthful generation irrevocably and yet, turn around to ask the youth to do what they, as leaders, had failed to inculcate and teach them by example.

Simply saying, 'do as I say and not as I do' does not wash with the current generation of the youths, and the leaders will have themselves to blame when the table turns on them, as it will definitely do at a point.

Kidnapping and Violent Crimes

Every nation has its own share of violent crimes and so do Nigeria. However, the astronomical increase of violent crimes, especially armed robbery and kidnapping in Nigeria, needs a particular attention because, it is a reflection of the inequity in the society, and hence, a reflection on the leadership.

I had always contended that where a few leaders arrogate to themselves all (most) of the resources of the land, a minority within the deprived followership will rebel violently against the leaders. Nigeria is beginning to see that in form of kidnapping and other violent crimes against the rich.

It is unfortunate that in the war between the deprived/oppressed and the oppressors, the successful hard-working individuals will get caught and entangled in the imbroglio. As the political leaders surround themselves with the security apparatus of the state and they become more difficult to target, the violent minority are targeting any affluent individuals who they sometime wrongly believe are politically exposed persons.

In Nigeria, the evil has been festering and being fermented over a long time by the corrupt and incapable political class who has been incompetent in developing processes and institutions that will ensure equity and fairness in dispensation of social justice and the justifiable dividend of democracy, better life, for its citizenry. The chickens are now coming home to roost and there is no hiding place for the failed leaders with or without their security apparatus.

That's just the way the cookie crumbles!

The average Nigerian politician does not understand that to ensure their own peace of mind and personal security, one should ensure the peace and security reigns throughout their community by ensuring, altruistic, purposeful and communal-benefitting governance.

Policing

Without being pretentious, Nigerian Police Force is one of the most corrupt and ineffective agency of government, both institutionally and on the individualistic basis. Having an understaffed federal policing force that is centrally controlled and expected to enforce all the laws of the country from common misdemeanour to treason and terrorism is not feasible, and it doesn't help the effectiveness and efficiency of the already corrupt and compromised force.

I support the clamour for state or regional police force. However, I will propose a regional or state police that is fully independent of the state governors. Commissioners of regional/state police should be elected on a 5year fixed term with no political affiliation and must have a verifiable policing or a relevant experience in security or defence units. Commissioner of Police will be responsible to an equally independent (directly elected or selected by an elected body like the legislature from across the spectrum of the local community) Police Working or Service Committee or Commission who will be responsible for the oversight of the police force.

The Nigerian policemen are poorly trained, unprofessional and archaic in their approach to crime detection, investigation and prosecution. Especially in the crime detection and investigation areas, Nigeria Police Force still belongs to the Stone Age.

The police force is not helped by the inept Internal Affairs ministry of the Federal government who is unable to coordinate and utilise the resources it has in an efficient and effective way to aid the police force in crime management. For example, Nigeria police force does not have a functional forensic and crime scene investigation department in any of its commands. Fingerprint and DNA technology are easily obtainable these days, and fingerprint technology especially, is still rudimentary with the carbon dabbing and lifting of prints which is not even a high technology by any standard. Nigeria has uncoordinated database of fingerprint that can be utilised for crime detection and management residing with diverse organisations like the National ID card authority, INEC, BVN etc. which in theory will cover over 90% of the country's adult population. Of course, a data protection law needs to be enacted to prevent abuse and misuse of data of subjects captured in the various databases.

It will also be cost-effective to capture the fingerprint and DNA of people arrested by the police and those with criminal convictions by the courts. It is a well-known fact and proven in various crime studies that up to 70% of reported crimes are committed by repeat offenders who have already passed through the policing or judicial system in one form or the other.

Fake News & Cyber Misinformation

Fake news and cyber chaos is here to stay, just like its offline and real life version. Nigerian education system, Information ministry and national orientation bodies need to step up and take their game to the next level. Fake news and associated cyber misinformation is another form of propaganda to undermine national peace and stability. The success of such campaign can only be gauged against the level of education of the populace who are the main target of such information.

Education, as mentioned earlier has to be outside the literacy and numeracy that is the norm, but extended to ensure critical thinking and ability to assimilate, analyse and evaluate information presented as facts.

Fake news and alternative facts are believed because people want to believe them or are unable to differentiate or process the wheat from the chaff.

Nigerians as I mentioned earlier, likes the impossible and will rather believe an outlandish tale than a mundane one irrespective of the source. Outlandish tales somehow tickles the fancy of Nigerians and solidly floats their boat to no positive gain; hence, rumours are easily spread, believed and resent in today's instant messaging and social networking circles where at the touch of a button, fake news can be resent to recipients in a phonebook numbering hundreds or even thousands.

There has been a clamour for social media to manage messaging within their network more, so as to reduce the proliferation of fake and alternative news. My humble advice to social-networking hosts or owners had always been the tagging of messages to know the IP of the originating source in their network. It easy to engineer, deploy and manage without causing much disruption to their existing infrastructure.

However, the war against fake news and alternative facts can only be won by public enlightenment and education. Rumours exist before the advent of the internet and will always exist; people must be educated on how to be circumspect of all the different news and information overload that they are bombarded with in our 24hr news cycle and social media messaging environment. It's a brave new information world, not exactly for the fickle minded!

Quota, Zoning and Meritocracy in Governance

Wherever all inclusive merit is displaced in place of quota or zoning for political expediency, there is ample evidence that such system are fragile and only need a slight tip at one end of the fulcrum to upset the equilibrium and the centre would not hold.

Inclusivity does not necessarily mean merit should be jettisoned or completely taken off the table when critical national decisions or appointments are being made.

My personal view is that zoning and all its variants of allocations of posts, resources, budgets etc. to balance the so-called regional representation and fairness is a waste of time and another one of the nails on the coffin that is slowly putting the Nigerian nation six-foot under. These claims are usually highlighted by politicians who are looking at political ascendancy for themselves into 'juicy' political appointments in Abuja.

The claims of lop-sidedness and imbalance in national apportionment of resources, appointments etc. are neither here or there. What Nigerians should pan for is the apportionment of resources based on needs and appointments to positions based on merits. With the rightly focused and detribalised Nigerians in the necessary positions, and a work-plan and policy guidelines in place, an overall competent Nigerian will outperform a sectional competent Nigerian chosen based on zoning or quota every time. No football team goes out to play a match using its second best team to meet a top class opposing team that is fielding their best team, why should a nation?

The world is such a competitive small village now, with ever shrinking resources to go round with every national governments looking at how to cerebrally get the best deals for its people and maintain a cohesive and progressive community, it's hardly a place to send your second or third or fourth best team to represent you. I, for one, as a Yoruba thorough-bred, will prefer a fair and competent ruler from any other ethnic group anytime than an incompetent Yoruba buffoon. And believe me all ethnicities in Nigeria have their own buffoons too!

Nigerians have to understand that the clamour for zoning, quota etc. is really a repertoire from the politicians' toolkit to ensure that they are invited to the table to have a stake and share in the spoil of the 'all juicy' Abuja bounty. It's never about representation of their constituents or the masses.

I, like all other reasonable Nigerians, do not care who rules the country as long as a level playing ground is provided for all citizens to pursue their aspirations in a fair, secure and egalitarian society.

The quota admission introduced into our educational system is also a system that destroys the basic requirement of progressive developmental strides in the educational sector, the need to compete and excel is stifled as the normal reward associated with success has been subjugated by the over politicised regional factor of quota balance in what otherwise should have been the driver of the economy and technological advances.

No economy that relegates itself to regional quota balance in its education sector, a sector that should be the driver of advances in the technology and the economy, in place of merit and excellence can truly become an economic powerhouse. Those advocating quotas, zoning etc. in Nigeria are just simply stupid, narrow-minded, selfish and myopic in vision to see the bigger picture. Where a section of a community is deficient or under-developed, the right approach is to pour extra resources to build the base of such section up from the ground rather than giving them tokens here and there to help individuals to get up the larder where they are unable to perform ultimately.

Niger Delta Militancy/Unrest

The Niger Delta Militants unrest and clamour for fairness is one freedom fighting or agitation that has never ceased to amaze me because of the strategy adopted. If your land is being contaminated by oil leakages, why exacerbate the situation by deliberately blowing up pipes to further contaminate and damage the land. Why go scorched earth?

The Niger Delta Militants strategy is short sighted and definitely myopic at best. Niger Delta inhabitants will have to live with the land long after the oil is depleted and the foreign people have left to the four corners of the world. It is prudent that the Niger Delta locals try to conserve their sensitive environment for the generations yet unborn.

It is imperative that the Federal Government ensures that the cleaning up of oil spillages in the past is expressly ameliorated and that gas flaring is curtailed to meet international standards. It is also very important that the private sector operators and joint venture partners in the oil sector adhere to internationally acceptable standard of code of conduct and practice. The lack of reputable standard and effective corporate social responsibility by the oil companies operating in the Niger Delta has been the bane of the disgruntlement of the people of Niger Delta, and rightly so.

The federal (including states and local) governments and the oil companies had also contributed in the restlessness in the Delta region by wooing the wrong type of leaders and self-appointed leaders who have lined their own pockets out of their own selfishness and greed in expense of the communal good, development and cohesion.

It can be aptly said that, with the resources poured into the Delta Region through the NDDC, Ministry of Delta Region and the 13% oil revenue derivative allocation to oil-producing states and local governments, nothing concrete can be shown for it except for creation of localised billionaires with no means or any proof of credible source of income. The people of Delta needs to rise up and hold their leaders and politicians responsible and stop the mediocrity of celebrating thieves who have stolen them dry in the past and yet throw some free crumbs their way, which they then celebrate as magnanimity by the leaders.

I, in my personal opinion, think the people of Niger Delta are misconstruing the importance of oil deposit with the agricultural achievements in the south east, south west and the north before and after independence. While no human can rightly lay any claim or contribution to the oil deposit that was consolidated millions of years ago in the Niger Delta; the cocoa, groundnuts and palm oil plantations created during the 50s and 60s agriculturally successful period were planted, nurtured and cultivated by humans with brawn, tears, sweat and blood. That was a story of human achievement over the odds, nature and the environment; and not harnessing of naturally occurring bounty of nature in the form of mineral resources.

Resource control may not be such a bad idea and I will support it, but with the crop of leaders that the oil-producing Delta areas have put forward to date, I can't see any cohesive use of the resource but a complete breakdown of law and order with each warlord and militant groups carving out their own little empire of the region. It will be an uncontrollable chaos. More workable will be a gradual increase of the current 13% derivative share to a threshold of 40%-50%.

Biafra Agitation

This has become a non-issue for now, as many of us suspected it was bound to fizzle out as soon as the latest progenitor, Kanu, lost the wind in his sail. That progenitor was a publicity-seeking nobody that managed to inspire unemployed riff-raffs' masquerading as authentic Biafra agitators. As expected, the progenitor disappointed all his supporters by abandoning them and their cause with the revelation that he was yellow through and through, yellow enough to disappear rather than stand up and be counted as a true leader should have done, when it really mattered.

Irrespective of the progenitor and the flash-in-the-pan performance, the Biafra agitation may be sidestepped for now but it will definitely rear its ugly head up sometime soon in the future. My personal view is that some Igbos may be nostalgic about the idea of Biafra, but common sense will prevail among the majority that realise that they have more to gain within Nigeria than without.

However, I believe the Nigerian government should give the Igbo people the opportunity to exercise their choice in a referendum, subject to the terms of the federal constitution or relevant amendments thereof.

A productive, peaceful and beneficial marriage has to be consensual and not enforced. And if I dare say, that is what most Nigerians want.

Boko-Haram Insurgency

The Boko haram insurgency is one that was created and nurtured by the incessant ignoring of social problems and other deprivations of the followership by the elites and/or leadership in the northern part of Nigeria, and coupled with the toleration of the simmering tinderbox situation by the seemingly 'secular' and unbothered federal government of Nigeria.

The Almajiri phenomenon fuelled by the mind-set of some people, and wrongfully reinforced by some community/religious leaders, in believing that conception and delivery of offspring is a gift from god and what god gives, god will take care of. And hence, they tend to hands-off and shirk their own parental responsibilities by failing to take adequate care and ensure that these offspring are socially, educationally and economically nurtured to face the vagaries of the present and very dynamic world. Absence of parental guidance meant these unlucky children get their education on the streets and are inevitably delivered into the hands of shady characters that will mislead, brainwash, misinform and use the vulnerable youths to do their own nefarious biddings including terrorism and the likes. This has led to the conveyor belt delivery of these hapless youths into the hands of terror recruiters and it is one of the primary roots and main sustaining breath of insurgencies like Boko Haram's. It is simple, no ready and steady supply of recruits, no insurgency.

Let's call a spade a spade. The problem with most uneducated or under-educated Nigerians, who happens to represent the majority and hence, most of the dogmatic people in Nigeria is dysfunctional nurturing and upbringing which invariably led to the pinning of their faith on charlatans who are proclaimed self-appointed representatives of God on earth.

As long as people realise that no human or mortal being on earth can truly prove that he has been anointed by God to represent him/er, or in the least be God's undisputable spokesman, all the so-called men and women of God are just self-proclaiming. I do not have any problem with self-proclaiming and for such proclaimer to have followership because they are guaranteed that right of association in the constitution and universally accepted human rights, however, it becomes a problem when their teachings and proclamation contradicts the letters of the Nigerian constitution which we all have arguably signed up for, to uphold and protect.

It behoves on common-sense that if 'western education' to gain knowledge and enlightenment is forbidden and sinful, then, usage of 'western manufactured arms' should equally be forbidden and sinful for gaining political advantage. One would expect Boko Haram to have utilized the age-old bow and arrow to execute their war in pursuit of their political aim. Nigerian government, on the other hand, have failed to engage and educate the general populace about the fallacy, flawed logic and ridiculous doctrine of the Boko Haram sect. Failure of the Nigerian government to carry out strategic information and propaganda to demystify the sect is a sure missing link in the complete annihilation of Boko Haram.

If I was cajoled to rule, the guiding rule of engagement and defence will always be pre-emptive; majorly, intelligence-led by infiltration of nefarious organisations like Boko Haram. It is a common mantra in military intelligence circles that attack is the best form of defence, and the mantra cannot be truer where one is facing an asymmetrical war like the Boko haram insurgency.

One can only gauge the success of one's intelligence apparatus with the number of catastrophes averted and those are not usually available to the general public. However, one can interpolate the decimated state of the insurgent and the number of their successful counter-attacks or suicide attacks to gauge the success of the Nigerian intelligence community. It doesn't look too good.

It is true; Boko Haram has been decimated militarily and is currently not in control of any geographical region or patch of land, yet, still being able to successful carry out guerrilla attack and infiltrate the hinterland and carry out suicide and other related terrorism attack is worrying and one needs to seriously analyse the support they are receiving internally and the complicity of some Nigerians.

Terrorism requires a lot of funds, logistics and support; and these are very difficult inflow of resources to hide. The intelligence community needs to do more to intercept the inflow of these resources. Financial resource is the oxygen of terrorism, cut it off and terrorists' leadership will have deserters and a revolt on their hands.

What has happened to all the known big-wigs and high-flying supporters of Boko-Haram as claimed by the governments from time to time? Nigerian leaders need to be serious and know the difference between politics and serious national security issues; that you cannot gain political mileage by using national security and safety as a bargaining tool should be sacrosanct and needs no reiteration.

Infrastructural Decay

Everything has been said about infrastructural decay in Nigeria, however, coming from a built environment background myself and having served decades in a more advanced country in that industry, where the maintenance culture is regimented and public infrastructures are well maintained, it is my opinion that what Nigeria had lacked were strategic planners. Although, you can also factor different other reasons like corruption, lack of continuity, lack of vision, warped maintenance culture etc.; failure to plan is the fundamental common thread that links all the other reasons.

I had always been an advocate of total life cycle costing for public (private as well) infrastructural projects worldwide. Embarking on a project requires that one ensures that the cost of the project and the related cost of maintenance for the life of the infrastructures are evaluated and accounted for at the conception/inception stage. Why spend N30M to construct an infrastructure and not allow or plan for the N120M that is necessary to ensure that it delivers the value and fitness for purpose required throughout its 20 or so years' lifespan?

It is pure stupidity and the bane of infrastructural development and efficiency in most developing countries like Nigeria that whole life cycle costing of public infrastructural projects has not be adopted and embraced entirely. It is also necessary to emphasise the associated need to create a sinking fund for maintenance which should be budgeted for yearly from the end of the defect liability period.

In total life cycle costing, the expected useful life of a public infrastructure is determined from the onset, based on past experience or the body of useful data available globally. It is assumed that the infrastructure will be renewed at the end of its useful life, hence it will cease to exist or maintained at the end of the useful life.

As a rule of thumb, the cost of putting up a public infrastructure is usually about 20%-40% of the total life cycle costing of the infrastructure while the cost of maintenance and servicing is responsible for between 60% and 80% of the total life cycle cost (discounting inflationary influence). That represents a ratio relationship between the life cycle maintenance and project costs of between 4:1 at the higher end and 3:2 at the lower end. I seriously doubt if the Nigerian story will any way conform to these norms.

Failure to plan is why a transformer provided for hundred houses originally was not expanded in capacity or number, to accommodate the connection of more than 400 houses. Failure to take into cognisance the fact that everything, including humans, deteriorates over time is why Nigerians fail to reflect on the importance of infrastructural maintenance and its ability to continue to provide a fit-for-purpose service throughout its useful life.

It is pertinent to say that failure to ensure adherence to civic responsibility by the authorities in terms of personal and individual tax payments inhibits the citizenry to take ownership of public infrastructures, demand proper maintenance for them and ensure fitness for purpose throughout their useful life. They simply do not care and do not see the infrastructures as theirs but that of the government as they do not see themselves as having any stake in those infrastructures.

It is apt to mention at this point that infrastructural maintenance must be locally available, both management and operational, and carried out preferably by the private sector preferentially because of their experience and position along the learning curve. This is contrary to the current practice, for example in the maintenance of federal roads around the vastness of Nigeria managed by FERMA from Abuja through their regional offices. Obviously, the state of all federal roads in the country attests to my view and vindicates it abundantly.

Erratic Power Supply

Normally, this should have been included under Infrastructural decay above, however, because of some particularly unique energy related points; I have chosen to address power related issues separately under its own sub-heading.

The dishevelled and erratic state of planning through the succession of governments in Nigeria cannot be more displayed in any sector more than that of power supply.

The three main sectors within the power supply value chain which are generation, transmission and distribution are bedevilled by their own intra and inter sectorial problems which are underlined by failure to plan by successive governments.

For years, despite the daily reportage of increasing population, it never occurred to anybody in the successive governments to plan for the expansion of power generation for the emerging new homes, commercial, industrial buildings and other power requirements of the exploding population.

Eventually, when it finally dawned on someone that the total energy production was inadequate to meet the power requirements of the exploding population and homes, new gas-fired electricity generation plants were commissioned with alacrity and all were happy. However, no one during the planning stage happen to realise that gas needs to be supplied to the newly commissioned gas-fired plants to work. Thus, when the gas-fired electricity plants were all ready to fire up there was no gas supply pipes and no gas supply contract in place; simply there was no gas to fire up the plants.

Eventually, through some ingenious government interventions whilst nobody was held responsible for the gas supply debacle, gas was supplied eventually to the gas plants and all were happy again. No sooner as the happiness sunk in that it was realised that no one again during the planning stage happened to realise that the old and decrepit transmission lines are unable to evacuate the electricity from the gas plants through the national grid. Now, gas supply lines are being constructed, gas supply contracts are being signed, gas-fired plants are being fired up, electricity is being generated but cannot fully be evacuated, transmission lines are being re-constructed to evacuate power into the grid. Yet, it has not occurred to anybody yet that distribution lines which forms the last mile of supply into the homes, businesses and other end users may not be able to carry the anticipated load.

Eventually, I am sure it will occur to another bright boy that the nation's grid of decrepit distribution network needs renewal and everybody will be happy again, actually, ecstatic this time.

The piecemeal way in which strategic planning of nationally important and critical issues like energy efficiency and self-sufficiency is handled without a forward looking broad overview of definite and possible scenario simulation is disheartening and frightening.

If I was cajoled to rule; sustainable, detailed and an all-encompassing strategic planning will be an order of the day for all government bodies and government-licensed private sector operators tasked with providing and maintaining our public infrastructures.

Proper and accurate metering of end users is also a fundamental flaw in ensuring that we are getting more for less, in terms of efficiency of the little strides in generation that we are making. With approximate billing, energy is consumed by users inefficiently; hence, the number of Megawatts that will normally be required to serve a neighbourhood of estimated billing electricity users will be halved compared to what is required to serve a comparable neighbourhood of metered (pre/post) electricity users.

I concur totally with the present government's initiative to separate the function of metering supply and installation from the core function of distribution by the distribution companies (Discos).

The stringent terms set for local generation needs to be looked at and made more achievable for small investors. Sale of excess generation to the grid by the consumers also needs to be looked at and the modalities need to be worked out for ease of entry, if only as a means to offset consumers' energy bills.

The unbundling and privatisation of NEPA/PHCN was a botched process in the first place with the distribution end getting the roughest deal. Concession were granted without due diligence with the concessionaires coming back to government on numerous occasions 'cap-in-hand' begging for subvention due to issues which could have been foreseen at the bidding stage.

I think the present approach by the present government is just trying to make the best out of a sector that was badly privatised in the first place.

Importation of Processed Crude, NNPC & subsidy

It is quite embarrassing to see a country that was self-producing and self-sufficient in petroleum products decline and turn into a state where it exports its crude oil only to import back the processed crude thereby denying itself billions of dollars in savings that could have accrued from non-importation of processed crude oil and thousands of jobs that could have been created for its teeming unemployed population. Basically, all the leaders of the country since the 1970s have contributed to the ineptitude in our oil industry, and are responsible one way or the other for the situation Nigeria found itself.

What is the rocket science in running a factory and ensuring that you follow the plant manufacturer's maintenance schedule to letter? Nigerians never cease to amaze me!

First of all, the government does not have any business running the 3 refineries in Warri, Port Harcourt and Kaduna; it is simply not their core duty nor do they have core competence in any case. These 3 refineries should be privatised and sold off to interested organisations with in-house technical knowhow and competence to run refineries.

With the technical know-how of some of the upstream partners- e.g. Shell, Chevron etc., it is not a rocket science to request contractually or by statue that all upstream partners should commercially refine a percentage (say 10%-20%) of all crude explored in Nigeria within the country. This will firstly save the country the capital cost of set-up and provide a technical expertise and transfer of technology that Nigeria require, especially with the extension of the remit of the local content act.

It is a fact that Nigerian oil resource is not well managed. Most Nigerians, in the know, agrees that the management of Nigerian oil resources, and indeed all resources, are in the least, incompetent, inept and rife with corruption.

Nigeria is a country where the exact data of amount of crude oil explored is not available (and where available, not accurate) nor is the agency tasked with representing the Nigerian people, responsible to the people; either directly or through its elected representatives. So, it is not unexpected if the populace kicks against the removal of fuel subsidy, especially when the perceived belief (rightly so) is that the country is rich enough to afford the subsidy despite the obvious corruption in the oil industry.

The PIB (Petroleum Industry Bill) being touted by its supporters as the panacea of all the petroleum industry problems is a mirage full of empty promises in so many pages of another set of bureaucracy and grammar.

My view is that NNPC should be scrapped and a more open, smaller and efficient organisation (in the semblance of the ever professional NLNG (Nigerian Liquefied Natural Gas Ltd)) set up as a replacement. After all, there is no rocket science in buying and selling, especially when you do not even need to open shop nor keep any stock!

It is a fact that PTS (petrol) is still being subsidised up until today well and below the international pump prices around the world.

My view is that subsidy in the current form is unsustainable and economically suicidal. I agree fully with other proponents that subsidy for production as against consumption makes more sense and these should be the way forward. For example, in the UK subsidy is on diesel used for agricultural productions and such diesel cannot even be used by the farmer for powering their private transportation as they are of different colouration from that used for transportation and have distinct colour in combustion. And the rule is enforced accordingly.

However, economic sense should be tempered with socio-economic situation and reality in Nigeria. This is a country where an average worker earns a monthly salary below N20, 000.00 and they will now be expected to spend about 50% of their salary on transportation to/from work. Hence, majority of Nigerians will automatically fall into fuel poverty which occurs when more than 10% of one's income is spent on fuel and fuel dependent services.

Despite my view that oil subsidy at the current level is not sustainable, I believe the government as a caring one will need to lead by example itself in carrying out demonstrable level of house-cleaning and belt-tightening in government before requesting that Nigerians should lose what most Nigerians believe to be their only dividend from the oil-rich country, subsidised fuel.

It is expected that a country should use their natural resources to enhance its competitiveness in the world market and Nigeria should not be an exception. However, if fuel subsidy would be used as a competitive edge, it should be for production of competitively priced tangible goods/services and not for consumption as earlier mentioned.

CHAPTER THREE -Policy Proposal

Introduction

It is imperative for any responsible government to manage and ensure the economic viability of the nation and the people therein. The assets, liabilities, revenue and expenditure of the state must be managed in such a way that it optimizes the return to the nation in the form of improved living conditions and standard of life for the citizenry. There has been a degree of hullabaloo in the country about the viability of all the states in the federation; it is my belief that the viability in most cases can be enhanced by much more innovative and outside-the-box thinking on the part of the various administrations in the federation.

It is my belief that the generally accepted belief in Nigeria that the civil service is a social service, and employment therein is the main means of alleviating poverty in the society is wrongly placed and the bane of the viability of all of the federating states. Public service or civil service in Nigeria, both at federal and states levels, are simply too large, unsustainable and does not represent value-for-money in any shape or form.

The civil service neither produces any tangible products nor services, hence, it contributes nothing factually to the GDP of the country in any form, yet, it gulps more than 60% of the budget of most of the federating states and the federal government itself.

It is an industry accepted fact in Business Processes Re-engineering (BPR) that any tasks, activities etc. that does not add value to a product or service is a non-value adding element and essentially, a waste. Exception occurs where the non-value adding task or activity is essential to maintain a standard or quality, such as accounting, quality control, sales etc. So moving a product from warehouse A to B without any attendant value addition by increased sale price is a waste in BPR terms. It is however not disputable universally that the essential non-value adding service, which the government represent in the Nigerian Plc., should not account for more than a digit point in the overall costs to any business. Nigeria's case is unique.

It is a well and generally accepted principle in governments around the world nowadays that a smaller government is more efficient and more effective. I will proffer ways to achieve leaner, efficient and more effective civil service, while ensuring that the social service factor is not lost and also, with positive contribution to the GDP of Nigeria at the same time.

The rightful place of the private sector in funding and provision of most facets of public service has been proven time and time again. With proper planning and implementation, there is no facet of government that cannot benefit from private funding and operation. However, I concur with the school of thought that believes that the wholesale privatization of all government functions renders the government itself irrelevant.

It is my view that Nigeria has not used enough private funding to carry out effective delivery of public services; hence, there is room for improvement in that respect. Where the government prefers to provide free public service to its populace, private sector can still be deployed as long as the service delivery is free at the point of delivery.

It is my view that a robust and vibrant private sector, which is recognized globally as the engine of growth in the real economy is highly required for stimulation of the economy of the Nigerian federation.

I concur with the clamour for reduced recurring expenditure of all governments in the federation; however, I differ by not agreeing wholly that all recurring expenditure is bad.

Nigerians abhors the high recurring expenditures on human resources that are not productive and I will maintain that recurring expenditures for maintenance of infrastructures and the built environment is key to our esteemed nation's way out of current global economic downturn. I dare say that the lack of adequate expenditure on the maintenance of key infrastructures over the years is a major contributor for the decay and the appalling state of the infrastructures and the built environment in Nigeria.

Civil Service (General)

As of now, I will like to believe that there is a consensus that the civil service, federal and state-wide, are way too oversized and needs to be trimmed. If I was cajoled, the size of the civil service will be reduced humanely by combination or all of the following ways:

Natural Wastage - Non replacement of retiring and depleting workforce due to death, job changes etc.

Voluntary Retirement/Redundancy - Retirement or redundancy due to inducement by the government because of job irrelevance.

Compulsory Redundancy - Retirement or redundancy due to inducement by the government because of job irrelevance.

Management Buy-In/Buy-out of MDAs - Commercially viable departments and/or units of MDAs can be privatized to existing staff to run commercially so their services is charged at the market rate to other MDAs and the public when they provide services. They may also provide their services on behalf of the government at no cost to the public i.e. free at the point of delivery, while the government pays the bill at previously agreed rates.

Verification/Validation of Staff - It is imperative that the federation and state governments, especially the federal government if I was cajoled, needs to validate and authenticate the actual civil service staff strength in the federal civil service. Biometrics capture of all validated staff should be employed and used as a basis for service provision to the civil servants.

A job study and analysis of all job functions is required to justify the usefulness of each specific job/post to the skills required to deliver the deliverables required from a department or unit of each MDAs.

It is imperative that the job study is done dispassionately by external consultants and redundant and/or irrelevant job functions identified and flagged accordingly. The expertise of specialized consultants cannot be over-emphasized for this function.

Various figures abound about the level of ghost workers and pensioners in the system; hence, to demonstrate value for money and operational efficiency to the citizenry, it is mandatory that any progressive government adopt a zero-tolerance to the existence of ghost workers and pensioners.

The offer for voluntary redundancies or retirement will normally be the first option, while compulsory redundancies will be as a last resort when a post is deemed to be an absolute waste on the resources of the state.

Optionally, the federal government can also create an internal competitive market in which all the departments/units within all MDAs pays for their inputs and then charges for their outputs after adding value within their respective departments/units. The department and units are also able to vie for business internally within their MDA or externally across all the state MDAs.

For commercially viable units/departments, the state should consider introducing management buy-outs by existing staff or buy-ins by external managers or operators with proven track record in the sector.

With the judicious implementation of one, combination or all of the above, 30% - 50% of recurring human resource costs to the nation can be reduced and such funds can be effectively positioned to provide a wider, more effective and efficient service delivery to the public.

Public Services

The place of the private sector in all the facets of public service delivery cannot be disputed. I acknowledge the attempt by the federal government to promote public sector involvement in providing public service; however, I regret to say that their vigour and achievements, in diversifying and seeking of avenues to reduce government spending, by use of the private sector to provide essential public services are few and far between. The bureaucracy attached to the process of privatization, PPP, outsourcing etc. is usually too onerous and cumbersome.

My view is that the following are all that are required for the vetting of privatization, PPP, outsourcing etc. and if I was cajoled, the process will be streamlined accordingly and the onerous existing bureaucracy scrapped:

- o Ability to provide the required services quantitatively and qualitatively.
- o Financial, manpower and technical ability to support service provision.

- o Flexibility, sustainability and scalability of service level and requirement.

- o Value-for-money for the taxpayers.

- o Agreement with workable service level agreements (SLAs), key performance indicators (KPIs) etc. etc.

I will now tackle my policy for each sector below. These are sectors that I know will benefit or have been proven in other governments to have benefitted tremendously from private sector involvement in public service delivery because of the knowledge base, experience curve and performance/result oriented attitude in the private sector.

Housing

The role of private sector in housing cannot be over-emphasized especially in the current revenue-challenging period facing the nation. The following are areas in which the private sector will add value, efficiency and effectiveness to the nation's housing policy. These will form the basis for my housing policy if I was cajoled:

- o Provision of Middle and low income housing for civil servants.

- o Ownership & tenancy. The private sector can be leveraged to provide the funding, building, sale/tenancy, manage and maintain mixed-use estates

- o Provision of Middle and low income housing for members of the public - Ownership & tenancy. The private sector can be leveraged to provide the funding, building, sale/tenancy, manage and maintain mixed-use estates

- o Provision of Social Housing for subsidized tenancy. The private sector can be leveraged to provide the funding, building, sale/tenancy, manage and maintain mixed-use estates

Health

Health is Wealth as the cliché goes. The health sector being a primary function of the government requires special attention. However, I contend that much more can be done for far less by the introduction of the private sector into some of the key areas of the health sector. They include the following:

- o Full or part privatization or outsourcing of all the frontline health functions while ensuring that the services provided by the privatized sector is bought wholesale (if necessary) or on an agreed rate by the government and free to any qualified member of the public at the point of delivery.

- o Provision of key non-clinical services in the federal medical centres/hospitals can be privatized or outsourced to reputable facilities management companies who will be able to add value by efficiency gains made through effective operations.

- o Provision of key clinical services in the federal medical hospitals can be provided by the private sector and delivery of such services more efficiently managed because of the learning curve achievements in the private sector e.g. medical & nursing services etc.

- o Provision of key medical infrastructures and equipment in the federal medical hospitals can be procured and maintained via the PPP/PFI model to ensure health professionals can concentrate on their core competencies.

- Provision of new specialist medical functions, like renal care unit etc. can be procured via the PPP model and existing specialist units outsourced to reputable private sector players

- Upgrade, Maintenance and Refurbishment of hospital facilities and infrastructures can be procured through PPP while the government can spread the cost accordingly without any huge capital outlay.

- Introduce nation-wide ICT powered record-handling system for general hospitals and health centres to maximize the efficiency gains offered by ICT and immediacy of service necessary at all health facilities.

Education

Education requires a special attention, and all will agree that the quality of primary and secondary education determines the quality of future adults groomed by these education systems which will shape the future of the country.

My primary view is that basic education up to JSS3 is important and the guarantee is already provided for in the UBEC acts, however, not every pupil is intellectually inclined, and some are technically more inclined while some are creative in nature. This diversity should be celebrated and supported by the type, quality and variety of education/skills acquisition that we give to our youths.

In as much as primary and secondary education are under the purview of the state governments, the federal government is able to set a national framework policy and I would propose as follows, if I was cajoled to rule:

- o The education sector will greatly benefit from public sector involvement. Indeed, new units in the sector can be procured, funded, built, managed and maintained by the private sector through private funding while the government only agrees the rate per student per year to ensure education is still free at the point of delivery.

- o Existing public schools can all be privatized whilst the government agrees to pay an agreed fee per student to maintain the education service is free at the point of delivery. This will ensure the private sector to provide good quality education with much more effectiveness and efficiency.

- o Upgrade, Maintenance and Refurbishment of Education facilities can be implemented through PPP while a suitable remuneration can be arranged with the private sector player over an agreed period accordingly.

- o Outsourcing of non-core teaching services in schools to free up teaching staff time for more productive work. Support services such as cleaning, catering and other similar services should be outsourced.

- o Provision of strategically located state-of-the-art technical workshops, ICT and science laboratories for the use of students (from colleges in a catchment area)taking technical subjects can be procured, funded, built, managed and maintained by the private sector. And nominal charges can be paid per student (or by the government where education is free) to the private sector provider. Technical staff can also be provided under the arrangement with the private sector provider.

- o Re-orientation of university education in Nigeria from grooming employment seekers to employment providers.

- o Re-focusing undergraduate and postgraduate thesis and dissertations towards commercially viable researches.

- o Reinforce the research and development institutes in the country and our universities to focus on commercially and economically viable researches by introducing robust and competitive awards/grants national scheme.

Commerce & Industry

The escalating numbers of unemployed youths and adults in productive age means Nigeria as a nation needs to look urgently at ways of stimulating the main engine of growth which has been recognized worldwide as the small and medium-size enterprises.

I concur with the more sophisticated belief that government is not and should not be the main source of employment, but as a facilitator that provide a conducive environment for enterprise to flourish.

I acknowledge the successful strive in the ease of doing business by the current government, however, I will contend that more tangible steps need to be taken, especially for SMEs. My recommendations below were bound to have come into place if I was cajoled to rule Nigeria. The following highlights a number of practical interventions to attract big businesses and incubate and grow more SMEs in the nation.

- o Provision of tax breaks/rebates/allowances for new manufacturing companies and SMEs setting up in the nation.

- o Provision of easy land acquisition and administration for manufacturing and other enterprises setting up in the nation.

- o Provision of a one-stop enterprise set-up agency to facilitate business set-up, cut red tape reduction and reduce bureaucratic bottlenecks.

- o Creation of business and manufacturing parks strategically around the nation with locally generated electricity through dedicated integrated power plant (IPP) and other infrastructures like good roads, water, security etc. These parks can be procured, funded, managed and maintained by the private sector with necessary government input wherever necessary to cut red tapes, land acquisitions etc.

- o Creation of strategically located bonded warehouse park with specialized storage services such as deep-freezer, cold room, bulk liquid storage, commodity processing etc. The park will also be facilitated with IPP, water supply, good roads etc. to ensure attractiveness. The bonded warehouse park can be procured, funded, managed and maintained by the private sector with government input wherever necessary.

o Provision of SMEs, Technology and Business Incubation Parks and Centres for new businesses; and the provision of subsidized and quality attendant support services normally required by small business from seed to expansion stage. The park can be procured, funded, managed and maintained by the private sector with government input wherever necessary.

o Provision of a single-digit expansion loan guarantee for companies achieving a specific investment and direct employment generation threshold in the nation.

o Provision of land costs subsidy for industries achieving a pre-set specific investment and employment generation threshold and targets in the country.

Employment Generation

Employment keys in with the preceding sub-heading, commerce and industry, and it is the primary concern of any government wishing to empower its people and ensure economic growth and stability to reduce the rate of employment to a single digit and wherever possible as closely to zero as possible.

Nigeria have realized that Agriculture should be the main-stay of the nation's economy, but to ensure effective maximum benefit to the communities, value-addition and processing of farm outputs will have to be expanded and supported initially by the government and preferably championed by the private sector.

In as much as funding for new enterprise is difficult to access by entrepreneurs, the government should still be the facilitator in employment generation. My recommendations below, if I was cajoled, are based on that premise:

- o Provision of turn-key manufacturing facilities by the government for a long lease to new and proven entrepreneurs or cooperatives. These manufacturing facilities will be initially targeted at producing low-tech materials usually used by the public sector and its contracted private sector partners e.g. Roofing sheets, tiles, nails, bituminous waterproofing etc.

- o Provision of turn-key agricultural value-addition factories by the government for lease to new and proven entrepreneurs or cooperatives e.g. cassava processing, cocoa processing, tomato processing etc.

- o Provision of strategically located turn-key cottage industries for long lease (or outright purchase) to proven entrepreneurs or cooperatives. These industries will be geared to provide day to day disposable, high volume items consumed by the government's MDAs, schools and other public sector institutions e.g. Paper-making, toilet tissue paper making, chalk making etc.

- o The government will ensure that public sector and government contractors' purchases are made from the clusters created under this subsection to provide a ready-made market base for the clusters. The government should create a fund for issuance of grants for innovative start-up businesses. The grant will be accessible to budding entrepreneurs through a transparent and competitive process that is open to all citizens of Nigeria irrespective of their educational or socio-economic or ethno-religious background.

- o Provision of youth resource centres for each local government which will provide a one-stop shop for youth guidance, career guidance, job-seeking, skills acquisition, networking, leisure, e-training and all other support needed for youth mainstreaming as defined by the commonwealth of nations and the United Nations.

- o Provision of graduates' re-orientation programme, to re-align graduates towards self-employment and development of entrepreneurial mind-set and skills, as against job-seeking.

- o The government should also set up a volunteering and mentoring scheme to help youths meeting a certain criteria in enhancing their workplace skills. The experience of the private sector should be harnessed into the scheme and suitably explored.

o The government should embark on comprehensive creation of database of all youths in the state, both employed and unemployed. Especially, unemployed database can be used for identifying skill sets for matching to available jobs around the country.

o Expansion of the very successful agricultural villages and settlements created during the first republic, albeit by private sector, with government-backed incentives and guarantees to ensure more effective and efficient operations.

o The government should facilitate the provision of high-tech farm machineries and equipment for the on-demand usage by farmers, preferably, through a PPP arrangement which is performance-based and driven by results. If required, the costs of the service can be on a pay-as-you-go basis, free or subsidized at the point of delivery.

o The government should facilitate the provision of storage, grain silos and other preservation facilities strategically across the country for storage and shelve-life elongation of farm produce.

o The government would encourage large scale and mechanized farming by cooperatives while facilitating financial support, guaranteed market price and linkages between large-scale farmers and proprietors of agricultural value-addition factories created earlier under this subsection.

o The government should provide advice to farmers by the use of agricultural extension workers and advise them on maximizing their yields and the crops which will give them the optimal yield in their own peculiar soil conditions.

Environment

The environment is fragile and needs serious intervention by the government at various level to ensure the survival of generations yet unborn. Nigeria would take a lead in Africa by bringing the environmental issue to the front burner by ensuring a significant reduction in the nation's carbon footprint.

o Promote and support use of electric vehicles and renewable fuel in government cars.

o Promote and support use of renewable energy and micro generation in government buildings.

o Promote use of renewable fuel in private cars and the use of public transport for most journeys. Also, emphasize the use of bicycle and construction of safe bicycle paths in urban areas.

o Promote and support (by subsidy) the use of renewable energy and micro-generation in private buildings.

o Promote the use renewable fuel for cooking and renewable portable solar light source (as against fossil-fuelled) during mains failure.

o Promote and support a strategic waste management system that emphasizes waste collection, separation and recycling.

o Promote the use of organic waste as fertilizers, and where applicable, use to fuel power generation in a modern carbon-capture plant.

o Provide strategically located waste separation plant (via PPP) that can separate organic, plastic, glass, metal and other wastes for recycling plants.

o Facilitation and provision of recycling plants in the cluster model as those mentioned in the previous subsection under 'Employment Generation'.

o Facilitation and provision of organic fertilizer plants from organic waste in the cluster model as those mentioned in the previous subsection under 'Employment Generation'.

o Facilitation and provision of waste-powered electricity generating plant with carbon-capture technology in the cluster model as those mentioned in the previous subsection under 'Employment Generation'.

Urban Renewal & Regeneration

Urban Renewal and Regeneration has been the mantra for the renewal of urban facilities and the regeneration of economic activities in the urban areas. While renewal (mainly aesthetics and functionality) itself can be marvellous, the integration with economic regeneration of the community has to be emphasized and underlined enough to have positive impact on the lifestyle and personal economy of citizens.

If I was cajoled to rule Nigeria, renewal of the built environment needs to be harmonized with economic regeneration by incorporating the following:

- Ensuring economic and business case for any urban renewal projects or proposals.

- Carrying out, on a case by case basis, health and safety evaluation to determine the impact and projected use of renewal projects on the populace.

- Where permissible, allow for regeneration impact assessment on the populace as a prerequisite to conception of urban renewal programme and projects.

- Provide strategically situated landscaped green parks as recreational facilities around urban areas.

- Enhancement and enforcement of signage and advertising laws. Enhancement and enforcement of built environment planning laws and regulations.

Transportation & Roads

A viable transportation sector (private, public and mass transit) is an underpinning requirement for any upwardly mobile economy and it is indisputably essential for growth and economic viability of all sectors.

Nigeria has seen major leaps and bounds in the transportation sector in recent times, especially during the time of the present regime with the revival in rail and upgrade of major inter-regional road links.

This success has been felt especially in the infrastructural developments, but not in the production of the rolling stock to keep the mobile workforce, goods and services in optimal deployment on a timely and efficient way. My stand, if I was cajoled to rule is to build on the solid foundation set to date and propagate the gains further down in the transportation sector chain by ensuring the following:

- o The renewal of the motor parks/stations across the nation in a model that is worthy of the 21st century. It will be piloted in a state and will be promoted to be replicated throughout the 36 states of the federation as a PPP venture through and through. The public sector should be invited to procure, fund, design, build, manage and maintain the motor parks.

- o In association with the FRSC, all the 36(including the FCT) states need to do a traffic audit and transport population in their respective state to aid in better designing and planning for transport related facilities.

o The state governments, in conjunction with the FRSC, will need to regulate commercial motorcycles (Okadas) by ensuring proper registration/licensing, training, testing, adherence to road safety codes and general operational code of practice.

o I believe there is a need for re-training or re-validation of all drivers in the nation. A proper testing and certification regime needs to be enforced and a mandatory psychological test required for erring drivers. This will have to be in conjunction with the FRSC and the enhancement of the state and national laws as may be applicable.

o Regional light rail networks will be explored, promoted and executed with emphasis on states and majorly private sector participation in any of its viable variant.

o Emphasis will be on the promotion of the local assembling of all rolling stock on the nation's roads and railways in the short-term; and expansion to full manufacturing in the mid-term range.

o New guidelines will be set on the proliferation of airports with emphasis on curbing unviable projects. Stricter guidelines and economic feasibility of proposed airports will be enforced to curb wastage of resources spent on underused airport facilities which should never have left the drawing board.

- o Wherever potentially possible, the federal government should explore the possibility of construction of new and maintenance of old road infrastructures through PPP/PFI model whereby the private sector will be procured to fund, maintain and operate the infrastructure, while their cost and ROI can be recouped back by directly charging the public for the use or where the infrastructure is required to be free at the point of delivery, charge the government.

Power

Power self-sufficiency, sustainability and scalability are the pre-requisite for industrialization in Nigeria generally, and indeed, in all the federating states of the nation (including the FCT).

Nigeria had started the journey well, but along the line many years ago, it lost its ways. The country failed to plan ahead to ensure that its energy capacity increases in line with its population and economic growth. It is a serious indictment of most of those who have claimed to be leaders of a potentially great country like Nigeria over the years and an indictment which will dog their legacies forever.

In addition to the gas-fired and other non-renewable generating plants, we will contend that Nigeria aggressively pursues a renewable energy generation and micro generation policy on the ground floor to forestall the inevitable tipping point of non-renewable energy dependency.

I propose as follows:

- Declaration of state of emergency in the power sector

- Immediate temporary augmentation of power generation with multi-fuel fired mobile power plant with about 50MW output per mobile unit per state, deployable and in operation within 180days (e.g. GE LM6000 mobile power plants). That will translate to 1800MW (1.8GW) within 180days.

- Streamlining of the bureaucracy and government red-tape for power generation will be a priority to ensure the lowering of the bar for prospective entrants into the power generation market while ensuring that the quality, viability, sustainability, scalability, safety standards, environmental issues and value-for-money are not compromised.

- Nigeria expands its current power generation plan by setting a target of about 30GW (30,000 MW) for generated power within the nation by 2025. I will target that 30% of the generated power should be through alternative renewable energy, micro-generation and excess private generation buy-backs into the grid from consumers.

- New consumer power pricing structure and template which reflects the actual cost of power production will be embraced to make power generation commercially more viable. Nigeria would further promote and enter into further PPP arrangements with the private sector to procure, fund, build, manage and maintain a renewable energy farm with a good return on investment in the nearest future. Of course, affordability will be a key, but subsidy at the point of delivery to economically disadvantaged people will be the norm instead of the exception.

- o Nigeria would also collaborate with emerging technologies such as the stored renewable energy concept currently in development by Dip-Holêr Management Co Ltd.

Water

Water is the sustenance of life and the provision thereof of drinkable water is one of the primary duties that all governments around the world owe to their populace. Hence, I feel it is paramount that we make my humble recommendation herein, if I was cajoled.

In Nigeria, I feel a wholesale and centralized provision of drinkable water to the populace via a centralized network of pipes and conduits is not sustainable at the moment, given the state of the old water infrastructures, cost of renewal and other associated developmental issues facing the nation and the state governments.

Taking into consideration all of the constraints, I will propose the following recommendations accordingly, if I was cajoled:

- o Promote states (including FCT) to commission a comprehensive study of water in their states, including natural water reserves, water availability, existing water infrastructures, ground water, surface run-offs, rivers, underground reserves etc.

- o Subject to the water study report, I will propose and promote that a dispersed water distribution system is adopted. This will involve a network of mini-water works wherever sustainable and a network of water reserves distributed around the communities for retail and industrial distribution.

- o I will propose and promote that PPP procurement route (in any of its variant) is embraced and necessary enabling legislation put in place to ensure revenue generation through judicious application of water rates and charges.

- o Indiscriminate creation of boreholes and wells need to be addressed and managed properly by the various state governments (including FCT). Apart from the adverse effects on the built environment, it also has implications on the underground water table and aberration in the flow pattern of surface water like rivers and streams.

ICT

ICT has proven in its few years of existence to be an indispensable technology that can be deployed to enhance productivity, efficiency and effectiveness in public service delivery, when deployed smartly.

From agriculture to energy to education, ICT has proven time and time again to be the indisputable champion of efficiency that was professed at inception.

However, despite the proven record, the take up of ICT at the federal level and the federating states has been slow and uncoordinated. A lot needs to be done in Nigeria by to make the business of the federal government, and indeed the states and FCT fully ICT-compliant to meet the challenges of the 21st century.

I identify the following as areas needing immediate attention:

- o Comprehensive IT implementation in all governments MDAs and networking of all government functions with attendant security, proprietary software, open/close source licenses and firewalls as may be necessary.

- o Creation of a digital archive and digitization of old legacy documents and paperwork for the digital archives e.g. building plans, survey plans, documents etc.

- o Migration of old processes and legacy systems (especially paper-based systems) to digital processes that can be powered by ICT and available on demand over the government network.

- o The government would aim to target, in the least, a spread of one properly networked computer per two administrative staff in the junior staff category and one computer per staff in the middle to senior staff categories.

- o To aid and ensure growth in the ICT sector of the country, the government would strive towards 100% localization of all ICT software deployed in the public sector and 50%, by assembly, of all hardware deployed in the short term.

- o Competitions will be held by government for all developers and software companies within the country to develop proprietary or open-source software for the government from time to time, but when adopted by the government, the copyright will be retained by the developer or Software Company for commercial purposes.

- o The government will promote the adoption of locally engineered software or hardware by the private sector either by subsidies, tax incentives or other incentives.

- o The government will promote and jointly fund with the industry, a globally recognized certification and testing organization for the Nigerian ICT industry that will guarantee the quality and safety of all ICT products (software and hardware) engineered or assembled in Nigeria, thereby ensuring export potential and trust is key.

Existing Infrastructures

It is a paradigm and a much debated and admitted fact that the lack of maintenance culture in the country is the main reason why infrastructures in Nigeria, which would normally be serviceable and functional, remain in a state of decay and rot.

Leaders generally like to leave a legacy of their time in office. However, unlike more advanced countries where the legacy is judged wholly by the electorates, it seems Nigerians prefer edifices which are usually abandoned by succeeding governments promptly on assumption of office.

I see the present government in the country as being progressive and with a 20-20 vision. The insistence by the current government to ensure continuation of moribund and abandoned projects of national importance in pace of newly commissioned projects is applaud-able. However, in addition to this, I believe maintenance of all government infrastructures and built environment should be paramount in the scheme of things to maintain their integrity and ensure that they continue to be fit for the purpose to which they were built in the first instance.

I will, if I was cajoled, propose as follows:

- Commission a comprehensive stock condition survey and asset audit of all infrastructure and built environment assets of the federal government of Nigeria through an independent, competent and professional private sector organization.

- From the survey and audit report, identify functionally viable and non-viable assets and strategically determine what to do with non-viable assets e.g. dispose, upgrade, demolish etc.

- Develop a costing of the planned maintenance programme (improvement, preventative and cyclical) for all built environment assets including all plant, machineries and services included in the asset register of the federal government.

- o Allow for inclusion, consideration and execution of all reactive/responsive and planned preventative maintenance programmes in annual budgeting and implementation.

- o Implement the principle of life-cycle costing for all major projects procured by the government either through the normal traditional method or through PPP/PFI or other arrangements.

- o Create an independent Asset/Facilities Maintenance Agency responsible for coordination of maintenance of all federal government built assets.

Security (policing)

Security is an issue which has dogged the existence of the nation in recent times and it is one of the critical criteria which dictate the cohesiveness of the community. Lack of security or ordinary perception of insecurity can turn neighbours into enemies and alienate communities which have hitherto lived, worked and played together.

A responsible government needs to ensure the security of its people is paramount and the community actually believes that their government is doing all that is in its capacity to ensure their safety.

I acknowledge the importance of security to the citizenry and the government's commitment to date; hence I will, if I was cajoled, do as follows:

- o Community policing is the buzz word in Nigeria at the moment in relation to state policing etc. however, the original concept of community policing is what I am proposing. It means "policing in the community with the community" whereby, everybody in an area knows and have a one-to-one relationship with the local policemen or women assigned to that community. It means the local policeman or woman is taken as part of the society and hence, he is intimated with the entire goings on in the community. I recognize that it takes time for individuals to be assimilated into a community as a local, hence, the argument for state/local police; however, I think this can be tackled by the next point below.

- o I propose the creation of Community Safety Officers (CSOs) by state police commands in the absence of state or regional police. The CSOs will have an overarching footprint in all communities of all the states (and FCT) and they will be required to work closely with the police. Of course, the CSOs will not be armed, but will have state-of-the-art communication gadgets to their base offices, police station etc.; and have no more than the ordinary power of arrest afforded to any other citizen of the nation. The CSOs will carry out the role of community policing by using effective modern communication, interaction and patrolling as their primary tools.

o   The spate of criminality in our urban centres and need for prevention, management and prosecution of arrested offenders necessitates the installation of closed circuit television (CCTV) in our urban centres. What I will propose to the states on this particular scheme would be of a PPP/PFI model. Funded, Installed and operated by the private sector while the government enters a long lease (with or without eventual transfer of the facilities) with the private sector operator directly or via the Security Trust Fund trustees as proposed below.

o   It is imperative that security is intelligence-led and the timely transfer of knowledge and information gained in the field is critical. Rapid information and knowledge transfer is imperative, and a dedicated radio communication over a secure channel is a must. All security operators including the Police and CSOs as proposed above should be issued with a two-way emergency radio for urgent and routine communications.

o   I will propose that the radio communication programme's funding, procurement, maintenance and management is done through a PPP/PFI either directly with the government or via the Security Trust Fund trustees being proposed below. The government or Trust Fund will then have to enter into a long lease with the private sector provider with or without an option of transfer at the end of the lease.

o   I still marvel at what is taken for granted in some neighbouring countries, not to talk of developed economies in terms of dedicated national emergency trunk line. Provision of a 3-digit emergency line is an international minimum requirement for reporting disasters, accidents and other emergencies world over. However, we note that there is no coherent national strategy towards the 3-digit emergency line; hence if I was cajoled, the government will strive to ensure the existence of a viable national toll-free 3-digit emergency line that cut across all networks and service providers in the country.

o   I acknowledge the mobility provided to the police by the Nigerian government over the years, in terms of cars and motorcycles, however in the urban centres, I feel that if developed economies around the world are still embracing age-old foot and bicycle patrolling by policemen and women, there must be a whole world of good in it.

o   I believe that the community policing proposed above will be more effective when combined with foot patrols and bicycle patrols, as most insidious criminality in the society is festered in the community and can usually be nipped in the bud at the community level.

- Although the creation of a security trust fund is not a panacea for all security threats in the community, it does give the state governments that implements one an additional bargaining power for tackling security issues affordably.

- The trust will be managed by independent and reputable fund managers, while the general community, individuals and corporate entities alike, are encouraged to buy into it as the stakeholders of security in the community.

- Overall improvement of professionalism amongst the rank and file of the Police is imperative. In the absence of state policing, the Inspector General of Police's (IGP) office in conjunction with the state government and the governors as the chief security officer of the states, engage the police state commands and to ensure professionalism of officers serving in their respective states.

- Bad behaviours such as carrying issued arms in mufti, non-tidiness, physical abuse of citizen etc. should be addressed with the state police management and IGP wherever possible to ensure the police act with decorum.

- A new unit of security anti-corruption will be created within the Internal Affairs Ministry, to tackle corruption within the police and other security organizations in the country with direct responsibility to the Minister of Internal Affairs.

- o Expansion of the whistleblowing policy to cover non-financial white collar crimes and the private sector.

IGR (Internally Generated Revenue)

Maintaining the status quo, internally generated revenue or IGR as the acronym goes is an aspect of governance which will eventually separate the men from the boys in the federating states in Nigeria.

The federal allocation to states with their ever increasing pulls from different contending aspects of the Nigeria state meant the allocation will reduce in real terms (with inflationary effect). It is mandatory, hence, that any state which wants to be economically viable and sustainable look inward and grow its local economy to boost local tax receipt. So, the federal government too needs to diversify from its mainstay of the mono-economy of crude oil.

I will have to acknowledge the good work currently being carried out by Federal Inland Revenue Services and its chairman by incrementally widening the tax net. However, there is always room for improvement and fairness in application of the rules of engagement.

- o Innovative and more out-of-the-box but fair ways of generating revenue, especially consumption/luxury taxes for individuals and environmental taxes for polluting individuals and corporate entities, should be targeted.

- o High net-worth individuals throughout the country needs to be brought right into the tax net urgently.

o The BVN is a verifiable tool that can be used
   to widen the tax net and identification of
   high-net worth individual; and it would be
   used as such.

Social Services and Welfare

A responsible government like the Federal
Government of Nigeria needs to provide a social safety
net for those who are vulnerable in the society. I
propose that a social services and welfare unit is created
to manage a structured social service and welfare
delivery programme in Nigeria.

o In other not to be abused, the government
   will need to identify what services will be
   delivered under its social programme, method
   of delivery, criteria for eligibility, scope of
   services, etc.

o A whole new range of professionals in the like
   of social workers, occupational therapists,
   home visitors etc. will be created.
   These are jobs which will have direct impact
   on the society and meaningful value-addition
   to the real economy of the nation. The

o National identity card will be made
   compulsory to access any government
   facilities and free-of-charge at the point of
   issue to all verifiable Nigerians.

o A birth to death identity tied to the national
   ID will be implemented to ensure availability
   and immediacy of service for all Nigerian
   citizens.

Legal/Legislative Framework

It is my opinion that legislation or further legislations may need to be enacted to bolster some of the proposals herein and render them practicable. Where similar or related law exists, there may be need for amendments accordingly.

- **PPP ROI Guarantee**

  The fear and reluctance of the private sector to invest in various big tickets and high profile public-private arrangements in Nigeria is borne out of the vagaries and non-continuity in government. It is a fact that most public-private investment arrangements normally spans over a number of years, normally for the private sector investor to have a meaningful return on its investment. Hence, it is imperative that a law skewed towards the guarantee of the terms of a PPP arrangement is in place to forestall any wilful termination of PPP contracts for any reason by any succeeding government of the day. And where payment is due from the government, provision should be made for guaranteeing such payments as a first line charge on revenue allocation of the government.

- **Personnel Transfer and Other Undertakings**

  A law needs to be put in place for the arrangements and transfer status of existing public sector workers when an existing service is to be privatized or managed under a PPP contract. This is very important as the welfare and benefits of existing personnel needs to be balanced and comprehended in terms of the new privatized service and structure of service delivery.

- **SLAs & KPIs**

Service level agreements (SLAs) and Key performance indicators (KPIs) are important to improving services and measuring the performance of the private sector in PPP arrangements. It can also be useful in improving and gauging the performance of different units of the public sector.

It is doubtful if a law is required or needs to be enacted to mandatorily introduce SLAs and KPIs as a useful tool in ensuring and measuring improvements in the service provision of the public sector or privatized services.

SLAs and KPIs are important management tools, and hence, some will argue that it should be issued as an executive order to senior managers/directors rather than enacted as a law or part of any enabling PPP acts. The latter position is preferable but the former will also suffice.

- **Regulatory Bodies for PPP by Sector**

There is a need to set up regulatory bodies for monitoring and performing oversight functions for PPP arrangements and privatized public sector services.

The regulatory bodies are not meant to interfere with the operational or strategic leadership and running of the privatized or PPP operators, but to ensure that SLAs, KPIs and other indicators that form the basis of the PPP contracts are achieved or exceeded. The regulatory bodies will also ensure that the privatized public sector service or the PPP operator operates within the confines of the framework that created it; deal with complaints from the public; adjudicate; collate performance; service effectiveness etc.

- **Employment & Contracting Local Content Law**

We also see a need for a law which prohibits, or in the least minimizes, capital flight from the nation by ensuring that local content is reflected in employment(public & private sector), government contracting etc.

The law will make it unlawful, or economically unviable, to employ non-citizen of the nation or issue government contract or work to non-citizen of the nation, where adequate and competent residents exists and are available to work or deliver the contract.

This proposal may be seen as protectionist, but protectionism is what every formerly underdeveloped nation like India, China etc.

used to lift themselves out of the doldrums of under development. Of course, exceptions will exists where the competency or specialism is such that no local organization or individual can be said to have the skills, capacity or technical know-how to deliver the contract. In my opinion, such situations will be few and far between.

- **Building Laws & Regulations**

I think there is an overwhelming case for a thorough overhaul of building planning laws and regulations.

The NBC 2019 (The Nigerian Building code) as it stands is inadequate and a technical guidance should ideally be issued alongside to back up the code and bolster the recommendations in the purely theoretical building code.

There had been many major building disasters in Nigeria in recent times and I do not see the trend receding anytime soon because, there are no visible steps being taken by the government to address the underlying problem.

Apart from the erection of structurally sound buildings, the buildings should be habitable and fit for purpose. Also, it should be ideally located in the scheme of its surroundings and general master-plan of the city.

It is my opinion that laws needs to be enacted and/or existing laws strengthened to ensure more progressive incline towards total professionalism of the construction and building trade with national vocational qualification required for artisans in the construction trade too.

My view is that Nigeria as a progressive society needs to have building laws which strives to improve its built environment (private & public) by enacting laws which will improve the quality and quantity of the stock progressively by insisting on a minimum standard for any new stock being added to the existing stock.

- **Environmental Laws**

Environmental laws needs to be strengthened and the use of generic Environmental Impact Assessment (EIA) currently in constant use needs to be discouraged and disallowed. The government should promote a project-specific EIA and enforcement of such throughout the nation.

It is a fact, for example that a lot of factories discharges contaminated, and in some cases hazardous, water into open sewers which then sink into the ground thereby contaminating the ground water and surface waters like streams, rivers etc. There is a need to strengthen the law and empower Environmental Officers to enforce environmental laws and prosecute offenders accordingly.

A law which emphasizes the safe disposal of wastes by individuals, organizations, private sectors, government etc. is a need at this critical development stage of Nigeria. Recycling of wastes wherever possible should also be one of the fulcrums that the law should be hinged on. The law should be the starting point for conservation of the environment and the basis of decisions taken for all government projects.

- **Transport/Traffic laws**

There is no state out of all the federating states in Nigeria that does not need an all-encompassing transport/traffic laws which will address the myriad of transport-related problems in the country. Nigeria too will benefit from a road traffic law/regulation that will codify what is expected from all public road users in the state, including pedestrians.

Amongst others, it will specify the regulation for motorbikes, bicycles, cars, other mechanically propelled vehicles and non-mechanical propelled vehicles. The regulation will also deal with registration of road users (including Okada riders) and enforcement of existing and new laws therein.

- **Maintenance of State Asset**

It is a generally accepted fact that the malaise and the rot in old built environment and public infrastructures in Nigeria, are primarily due to lack of maintenance and lack of general maintenance culture. In Nigeria, structures and infrastructures which have not reached the end of their service life normally are rendered non-serviceable because of lack of maintenance.

As a starter, I will propose a law which entrenches planned maintenance of all public facilities and infrastructures in the public sector and makes the responsible public officer criminally accountable for neglect of any public facilities or infrastructure (likened to wilful damage of public facility/infrastructure). Needless to say, good maintenance culture (both reactive and planned) elongates the serviceable life of these public facilities/infrastructures and makes economic sense on the long run.

The law may be extended to the private sector to ensure a continuously improving built environment which will serve and ensure sustainability of our dwellings in Nigeria.

It is mandatory in some advanced economies that the authorized bodies empowered by planning laws are able to issue fines, prosecute or exercise a compulsory purchase order or demolish private sector infrastructures that had fallen into a state of disrepair to the extent that it constitutes health and safety hazard to the general populace.

• **Health and Safety**

I also see a need for a comprehensive health and safety regulation for workplace and public spaces. The legislation may create an executive agency tasked with carrying out an oversight function and regulatory duties to enforce the legislation which will be all encompassing for various industries, workplaces and construction sites. The legislation will be required to tackle the need for risk assessment of various hazards which are present in the applicable space.

In as much as health and safety is an on-going issue and it is not usually possible to eliminate all possible risks in the workplace, it is necessary for the legislation to proffer steps in form of risks management systems to mitigate or minimize these risks. Usually the regulatory agency tasked with managing the legislation will develop and issue an Approved Code of Practice (ACoP) for each industry.

• **Disabled, OAP & Minors etc. Discrimination and Associated laws**

I will propose that a disability discrimination act should also be enacted in the nation (this has now been signed into law in the first quarter of 2019) to ensure non-discrimination of disable and other physically challenged individuals.

A separate act of the assembly may be needed as an all-encompassing protection law for all minority groups including old aged pensioners (OAP), Minors, ethnic minorities etc. in the community.

This law or act of the house of assembly will further promote inclusion of these vulnerable groups in the society. In developed economies like the UK, PWDs (people with disabilities) account for about 20% of the population, hence, 20% of the economy and 20% of the purchasing power. No reasonable government or indeed, any corporate entity can ignore the economic muscle of that segment of the society.

- **Data Protection**

The advent of ICT and data warehousing by some service providers, organizations and government agencies e.g. telecoms, co-operative societies, pension schemes etc. necessitates the need for a data protection act or law which will define under which conditions individuals data kept on their system is shared with third parties and other data users. The law should deal with the data owner, data controller, consent required, data management, data manipulation etc.

With the myriad of personal data being warehoused by different agencies like the

CBN, NPC, INEC, etc. for BVN, National ID, electoral list etc. respectively, there arises a need to have an independent data protection agency to ensure that these data are used solely for the purpose for which it was obtained.

EPILOGUE

Of course, nobody will cajole me or anyone to rule in Nigeria with so many desperate up-takers in the wing for the job, but even if I was cajoled, I will flatly refuse not because of lack of ability but because of lack of interest and a lethargic followership that are too much set in their collective delusional psychosis.

However, we Nigerians have a habit of complaining and not proffering solutions because of the fear of being seen as stupid or politically incorrect in our views, hence the impetus for this book. My take is quite different, the wackier the idea, the more it can be tweaked to provide an out-of-the-box solution to a fettering and insidious problem.

My attempt in this book is to look at the common things that the average Nigerian grumbles about on a daily basis and apply not-so-complicated solutions to tackle those needling issues. The ideas proffered herein is not exhaustive and shouldn't under any circumstances be taken as the holy grail, it's meant to be a catalyst to get the leadership and followership to think of innovative ways to get the Nigeria nation working like we all would prefer.

This may not be a prescribed handbook for Nigerian politicians or public servants nor a recommendation for scholarly work, but I do hope that it will instigate that leadership class of Nigerians of all persuasions and the public at large to stop being passive by becoming more proactive about fixing the ills in the Nigerian society. All hands have to be on the deck to ensure an egalitarian and better society where communal caring for our fellow Nigerians is the norm rather than the exception.

Of course, we will always have the greedy and the selfish amongst us. Greed and selfishness are both undesirable human traits that are, as at yet, not been able to be bio-genetically isolated from the human genome, however, it is my hope that this book will inspire Nigerians to ensure that those greedy and selfish amongst us never get to climb to that excelled position of leadership, simply by ensuring positive use of their electoral rights and devolving themselves from the 'You chop I chop' or 'Us against them' mentality of the average Nigerian in their choice of political leaders.

Merit should be the order of the day and all other issues argued and raised by politicians like ethnicity, religious leaning, political pedigree, social background etc. are just red herring to distract Nigerians from the real issues. Those politicians use those distractions to gain local support and ensure their own relevance in national politics.

Most of the problems facing Nigeria as a nation are mainly institutional and individualistic in nature; they are not insurmountable with a set of dedicated leaders elected on merit and credibility, who are trustworthy enough to lead from the front by doing what they preach. Nigerians should also emphasize and insist on better governance, and wherever necessary, constructive criticism of their leaders by proffering solutions to problems rather than just complaining. No single leader can turn Nigeria, a nation of over 180million people, around alone. All hands must be on deck to ensure an egalitarian, fair and equitable society where dreams can be achieved by any individual irrespective of their background by pure hard work, ingenuity and perseverance.

The leader and his/er government must however, ensure national education and orientation to ensure that ordinary Nigerians buy into the vision and ensure that all efforts are focused and synergized towards a common goal.

That is my piece.

Acronyms
(in the order of appearance)

ICT - Information and Communication Technology
IGR - Internally Generated Revenue
PPP - Public/Private Partnering or Partnership
ROI - Return on Investment
SLA - Service Level Agreement
KPI - Key Performance Indicator
OAP - Old Aged Pensioner
MDA - Ministries, Departments and Agencies
RMFC - Revenue Mobilisation and Fiscal Commission
KISS - Keep It Straight/Short and Simple
FERMA – Federal Roads Maintenance Agency
NFIU - Nigeria Financial Intelligence Unit
NGF - Nigerian Governors' Forum
INEC - Independent National Electoral Commission
UN - United Nations ID - Identification
BVN- Bank Verification Number
DNA – Deoxyribonucleic Acid
NDDC- Niger Delta Development Corporation
OPADEC – Oil Producing Areas Development Commission
(States)
DisCos - Distribution Companies (Electricity)
NEPA - National Electric Power Authority
PHCN - Power Holding Corporation of Nigeria
NNPC – Nigerian National Petroleum Corporation
NLNG - Nigerian Liquefied Natural Gas
BPR - Business Process Re-engineering
GDP - Gross Domestic Product
PFI - Private Finance Initiative
JSS3 - Junior Secondary School (level 3)
SME - Small to Medium Enterprise
IPP - Integrated Power Plant
FRSC - Federal Road Safety Corps
FCT - Federal Capital Territory

IT - Information Technology
CSO - Community Safety Officer
CCTV - Closed Circuit Television
IGP - Inspector General of Police
NBC - Nigerian Building Code
EIA -Environmental Impact Assessment
ACoP - Approved Code of Practice
UK - United Kingdom
PWD - People with Disability
CBN - Central Bank of Nigeria
NPC - National Population Commission

www.ingramcontent.com/pod-product-compliance
Lightning Source LLC
Chambersburg PA
CBHW031127250726
48655CB00002B/546